Law Essen

# EUROPEAN LAW

Law Essentials

# EUROPEAN LAW

Stephanie Switzer, LL.B. (Hons)

*Lecturer in Law, formerly of
the University of the West of Scotland
and now of
the University of Dundee*

DUNDEE UNIVERSITY PRESS
2009

First published in Great Britain in 2009 by
Dundee University Press
University of Dundee
Dundee DD1 4HN

www.dup.dundee.ac.uk

ISBN 978 1 84586 009 7

No natural forests were destroyed to make this product;
only farmed timber was used and replanted.

*British Library Cataloguing-in-Publication Data*
A catalogue record for this book is available on request from the British Library

Typeset by Waverley Typesetters, Fakenham
Printed and bound by Bell & Bain Ltd, Glasgow

# CONTENTS

# TABLE OF CASES

Page

# TABLE OF STATUTES

# TABLE OF EUROPEAN LEGISLATION

## Treaties and Conventions

Page

## Directives

# 1 THE "MAKING" OF THE EUROPEAN UNION

This book is designed to provide a basic framework for the study of the law of the European Union. The Union of today enjoys competence to make law in a wide range of areas, from environmental protection to agricultural policy. This competence to make law in such a wealth of areas is the result of many years of building and promoting European-level co-operation and integration. This book will explore the legal development of the European Union and thereby provide an *essential* framework for the study of European law.

## THE BEGINNING OF THE EUROPEAN INTEGRATION PROJECT

Understanding the law of the European Union requires knowledge of the manner in which the Union came into existence. The history of the European Union can be traced back directly to political develop-ments after the Second World War. Following the cessation of hostilities in 1945, a spirit of co-operation emerged among the countries of Western Europe. This mood of solidarity reflected the shared desire of Western European countries such as France and Germany that such a war should never happen again. Accordingly, various proposals were put forward to promote both economic and political co-operation between the countries of Western Europe. The idea behind this co-operation was that if countries were tied together both economically and politically, this would help to secure a peaceful future.

## THE CREATION OF THE EUROPEAN COAL AND STEEL COMMUNITY (1951)

The spirit of solidarity was cemented in 1951 by the formation of an organisation called the European Coal and Steel Community (ECSC) with France, Italy, Germany and the three Benelux countries (Belgium, Luxembourg and the Netherlands) as members. The ECSC was formed as a result of a report by the French Foreign Minister, Robert Schuman, which proposed to put the production of coal and steel resources in Europe under a central authority independent of state control. A state's ability to wage war at that time was dependent upon its capacity to produce coal and steel. By tying the production of these resources to a centralised authority, the ability of states to go to war would be reduced. The institutions set up under the ECSC included a High Authority (this body would later become known as the Commission), a Council of Members and an Assembly composed of appointees from national parliaments. Disputes were to be settled by a Court of Justice which was tasked to ensure the observance of the Member States to the provisions of the Treaty. The formation of the ECSC represented an important milestone in the process of European integration, although it no longer exists, having expired in 2002 after 50 years.

## THE FORMATION OF THE EUROPEAN ECONOMIC COMMUNITY AND EUROPEAN ATOMIC ENERGY COMMUNITY (1957)

Following the formation of the ECSC, its six Member States continued to discuss what moves they could put in place to promote *further* European integration. These negotiations culminated in the creation in 1957 of an organisation called the European Economic Community (EEC) and a body called the European Atomic Energy Community (Euratom) which aimed to promote European co-operation in the field of atomic energy. Both these Communities followed the same institutional structure as the ECSC, although only the Court of Justice and Assembly were shared by all three Communities.

While the establishments of each of these Communities were important milestones in the development of European integration, the formation of the European Economic Community was undoubtedly the most significant in terms of its impact upon the future of Europe. The most important elements of the EEC Treaty are considered below:

- The original Treaty establishing the EEC, sometimes referred to as the Treaty of Rome, was concerned mainly with economic co-operation.

- However, the EEC Treaty also contained a political agenda which is apparent from Art 2 of the original EEC Treaty. This noted that the integration of the economic policies of Member States would lead to "closer relations between the States belonging to it".

- Thus, while the initial aims of the EEC Treaty were primarily to assist in the process of European economic co-operation, it was recognised that such co-operation could "spill over" into other areas and so lay the foundations of an "ever closer union" between the peoples of Europe.

## THE EEC INSTITUTIONS AND GOVERNANCE STRUCTURE (1965)

The next important step on the road to further integration in Europe was the creation of the so-called Merger Treaty. In this Treaty, signed in 1965, it was agreed that the EEC, the ECSC and Euratom would share the same institutions. Before that, the EEC, Euratom and the ECSC shared a Court of Justice and an Assembly but otherwise retained separate institutions. The Merger Treaty helped to ensure continuity of governance across each of the three communities, thereby assisting the process of European integration.

## THE LUXEMBOURG ACCORDS (1965)

In 1965, a major crisis occurred within the EEC. This crisis is interesting as it underscores the tensions which existed at the time between the different Member States regarding the pace of the European integration process. This tension pivoted around discussions regarding the way in which decisions were made.

Some states who were members of the EEC were in favour of "supranational" decision-making processes while others were in favour of "intergovernmental" decision-making structures. Intergovernmentalism is the usual way in which decisions are made on the international level. In such a system, all states must agree before a decision is made. As such, states retain their power of veto over key decisions which affect their national interest. However, in a supranational system, states relinquish some of their power to say "no". A feature of a supranational system is thus majority (rather than unanimous) decision-making structures. Under such a system, not all states have to agree in order for a decision to be brought into force.

The crisis which erupted in 1965 was focused upon the tension between supranationalism and intergovernmentalism. In response to a proposal for majority voting to replace unanimity in certain areas of EEC competence, the French delegation refused to attend certain meetings. Only after 6 months was the stalemate broken with the adoption of an informal agreement called the Luxembourg Accords. As a result, unanimous voting became the main way of adopting EC legislation. With the agreement on the Luxembourg Accords, the effective dominance of intergovernmentalism considerably slowed the pace of European integration until the 1980s with the introduction of the Single European Act.

## THE SINGLE EUROPEAN ACT (SEA) (1986)

The Single European Act was signed in February 1986 and came into force in June 1987.

### Background to the Single European Act

The late 1970s was a difficult time for Europe both politically and economically. In political terms, the process of European integration had gone somewhat awry. Economically, Europe was losing its international competitiveness and suffering the effects of the economic turmoil caused by the two oil crises of the 1970s during which the price of oil rose considerably.

By the early 1980s, an improved economic situation and the arrival on the scene of pro-integration European politicians sparked a revival of the European political project. At the same time, it was recognised that action on the economic front would help promote the competitiveness of Europe against increased Japanese and United States' competition.

### What did the Single European Act do?

The Single European Act was designed to "complete the Internal Market" by 1992 and so move the European Economic Community beyond a simple customs union (in which there are no internal barriers to trade in the form of tariffs or customs duties) to an area with almost *complete freedom of economic activity* characterised by the free movement of people, goods, services and capital.

Furthermore, the SEA ushered in a change to the voting procedures in the EEC so that many more decisions could be taken by supranational methods using a process termed "qualified" majority voting. The SEA also introduced changes that meant that in certain areas the Parliament had a larger role in the legislative process (through the adoption of the so-called co-operation procedure outlined in Art 252 EC). In addition, the SEA extended the Community's legislative competence to areas such as health and safety at work, economic and social cohesion and research and technological development. Overall, the significance of the SEA cannot be overemphasised. Its goal to create the "internal market" by 1992 set in motion a chain of initiatives which ultimately helped to shape the European Union of today.

## THE TREATY ON EUROPEAN UNION

The Treaty on European Union (TEU) was signed in 1992. It is commonly referred to as the Maastricht Treaty.

### What changes did the TEU bring about?

#### The creation of the European Community

The TEU renamed the European Economic Community the European Community. Accordingly, the Treaty establishing the EEC was renamed the European Community (EC) Treaty. When Articles of the EC Treaty are referred to in legal texts, they will often be written as "Art [number] EC".

#### The extension of the aims of the Community

The TEU amended the aims and competences of the Community to include areas such as social and environmental protection as well as economic and monetary union.

#### Introduction of the "co-operation procedure" (Art 252 EC) to more areas of decision making

More detail on the way in which law is made within the Community will be provided in Chapters 4 and 5. However, at this juncture it is important to note that the introduction of the so-called co operation procedure had the effect of increasing the involvement of the European Parliament in the legislative process. This is significant as Members of the European Parliament (MEPs) are directly elected by European citizens. Increasing their involvement in the legislative process therefore helps to ensure that the way in which law is made within the Community is more democratic.

#### Introduction of the co-decision (Art 251 EC) procedure for making legislation

This procedure grants the Parliament an even greater role in the legislative process than the co-operation procedure.

#### The creation of the European Union

Perhaps the most significant change ushered in by the TEU was the creation of the European Union (EU). The aim behind the creation of the EU was to build a "three-pillared" structure comprising the following areas:

- **Pillar I**: The European Coal and Steel Community, Euratom and the EC. This pillar is called the EC pillar. Most of the discussion in this book will be concerned with law made under this first pillar.
- **Pillar II**: The Common Foreign and Security Policy (CFSP) pillar. This pillar was intended to promote co-operation between Member States in pursuing common policies with the rest of the world.
- **Pillar III**: Justice and Home Affairs. This pillar was instituted to bring about co-operation between Member States in areas such as policing, criminal matters, immigration, asylum and border controls.

### Are the decision-making structures the same across each pillar?

As outlined above, the Treaty of European Union created the "European Union" composed of three pillars, with each pillar having different legislative competences and decision-making structures. Broadly, the EC pillar was much more supranational than Pillars II and III. Decision-making structures in Pillars II and III were more intergovernmental in nature with less of a role for the Parliament, the Commission and the Court.

### Why was this three-pillar structure created?

Broadly, while Member States wanted to co-operate in areas such as immigration, border control and policing, they did not wish to relinquish formal control over these areas to supranational decision-making structures. This is because issues such as co-operation in criminal matters concern very sensitive areas of national policy which are considered to be at the very heart of national sovereignty. The pillar structure is therefore useful to achieve such co-operation as it allows different decision-making structures to be utilised in accordance with the issue under discussion.

### THE TREATY OF AMSTERDAM (1999)

The Treaty of Amsterdam was signed in 1997 and entered into force in May 1999. It has been described as a "consolidating Treaty", its main substantive purpose being to bring Europe closer to its citizens by making it more relevant to them. While the Treaty of Amsterdam was originally intended to remodel the Union in time for the expansion of its membership in 2004, its effects were far more modest.

## What changes did the Treaty of Amsterdam bring about?

### Pillar I

- The EC pillar was "cleaned and tidied up". This effectively meant that the numbering of the EC Treaty was changed and obsolete provisions were removed. It is important to note that some legal cases will refer to the old numbering of the Treaty when referring to specific Treaty Articles. It is vital to remember this when reading judgements delivered before the introduction of the Treaty of Amsterdam.

- Use of co-decision legislative procedure was expanded to other areas of the EC's legislative competence. At the same time, the procedure itself was amended to help ensure the increased involvement of the European Parliament in the legislative process.

- New areas of competence were granted to the EC such that it now has the power to make legislation to combat discrimination on the grounds of race, ethnicity, age, disability, sex and sexual orientation.

- Issues such as visas, asylum, immigration and customs co-operation, previously under the remit of Pillar III, were also transferred to Pillar I.

### Pillars II and III

The main changes occurred under Pillar III, which was renamed "Police and Judicial Co-operation in Criminal Matters" to reflect the transfer of some of its competences to Pillar I.

Overall, the Treaty of Amsterdam was meant to prepare the Union for the enlargement of its membership. However, it failed in this task, leaving the main details to be sorted out by the subsequent Treaty of Nice.

## THE TREATY OF NICE (2000)

The Treaty of Nice was signed in 2000 but did not enter into force until 2003. The reason for this delay was the rejection of the Treaty by the Irish electorate following the results of a referendum on the question of ratification of the Treaty. The Irish were subsequently given a second chance to vote on the Treaty, in which the results of the first referendum were reversed and ratification agreed to.

The main function of the Treaty of Nice was to bring about the institutional and structural changes necessary to bring about the enlargement of the EU. Changes introduced by the Treaty included a reorganisation of the Commission as well as an increase in the number of Members of the European Parliament to a maximum of 732. The influence of the Parliament over the legislative process was also enhanced, with the use of co-decision extended to more areas of Community competence. Additional amendments were made to the voting procedures in the Council, with more issues subject to qualified majority voting rather than the requirement of unanimity.

## INCREASE IN MEMBERSHIP OF THE EU

In 2004, the membership of the EU increased from 15 members to 25 with the admission of 10 new Member States. In January 2007, the membership of the EU again increased with the accession of Bulgaria and Romania. Future enlargement is likely, with Croatia, the Former Yugoslav Republic of Macedonia and Turkey each actively seeking membership. More detail on the enlargement of Europe will be provided in Chapter 2.

## CONSTITUTIONAL TREATY FOR EUROPE

The next significant step in the process of European integration was the drafting of a Constitutional Treaty for Europe. This Treaty is, however, dead.

The so-called Constitutional Treaty emanated from a 2001 summit of the European Union. This summit, called the Laeken summit, produced a Declaration on the Future of the European Union which posed a series of questions about the future of the EU. These questions centred upon issues such as the division of competences in the EU, simplification of law-making structures, how to deal with the perceived "democratic deficit" within the EU and, in a related sense, how to make the EU itself more transparent, democratic and effective. A fundamental concern addressed within the Declaration was the need for the various European institutions to be "brought closer to the citizen". A body, called the Convention, was assigned the task of drafting a Constitutional Treaty for the EU which would help address the concerns posed in the Laeken Declaration.

The Convention finished its work in 2003 but, as a result of disagreement between Member States on issues such as the allocation of votes within the Council, the resultant Constitutional Treaty was not signed until October 2004. The Constitutional Treaty was intended to "simplify" the structure of law making within the EU. This involved dissolving the pillar structure and providing for more areas to be decided on the basis qualified majority voting rather than unanimity. The competence of the EU was to be extended to more areas of law making and an explicit statement was included on the primacy of EU law over national law (see Chapter 6). More significantly, if the Treaty had entered into force it would have replaced the existing Treaties with a single, all-encompassing text.

In mid-2005, France and the Netherlands put the proposed Constitutional Treaty to a referendum. However, in both countries, their populations voted "no" to the Treaty. While some 13 other countries eventually ratified the Treaty, its rejection in France and the Netherlands resulted in the EU Member States opting to undertake a "period of reflection" after which it was agreed that the Constitutional Treaty was dead.

It is arguable that the fatal mistake of the drafters of the Constitutional Treaty was to title the document as a "constitution". While certain state-like features such as an official Union anthem, motto – "United in Diversity" – and flag were to be introduced by the Treaty, for the most part it represented little more than a reorganisation of the European legal order. However, it is arguable that framing the Treaty as a constitution was a significant contributing factor in its subsequent failure.

An important point to remember is that the Constitutional Treaty never became law as a result of its rejection by the French and Dutch electorate. A similar fate may be suffered by its successor, the Lisbon Treaty.

## THE TREATY OF LISBON

After the Constitutional Treaty was declared dead, an Intergovernmental Conference was convened in the summer of 2007 to thrash out the document intended to replace the Constitutional Treaty. The resultant Treaty was put to the European Council at a meeting in December 2007 in Lisbon, Portugal. After limited discussion, the text of what is now referred to as the Lisbon Treaty was adopted. The Lisbon Treaty is not yet, however, law. It will only become law if adopted by all the Member States.

### What is the basic structure of the Treaty of Lisbon?

The Treaty of Lisbon provides that the European Union will be based upon two Treaties: the Treaty on European Union (which will be amended) and the Treaty on the Functioning of the European Union (TFEU) which is effectively an amended and renamed version of the EC Treaty.

While the Treaty of Lisbon is not as ambitious in its aims as the Constitutional Treaty, its introduction will bring about a number of changes in the European legal and political order. The most fundamental of these are listed below.

## Key changes under the Lisbon Treaty

If adopted, the Lisbon Treaty will bring about the following key changes:

- help to demarcate the boundaries of legislative competence between Member States and the Union;
- ensure the accession of the EU to the European Convention on Human Rights (ECHR);
- make co-decision the "norm" for EU legislation and thereby grant the European Parliament a far more equal role in the legislative process;
- extend qualified majority voting to more areas;
- remove the distinction between the European Community and the European Union;
- dismantle the "pillar structure", although specific procedures will be put in place for decision making under CFSP;
- introduce a new High Representative for the Union in Foreign Affairs and Security Policy who will also act as Vice-President of the Commission and will be assisted in this role by a new "European External Action Service";
- give the European Union legal personality so it can negotiate agreements with third countries and international institutions;
- introduce the role of "Council President", a position which will be held by the appointee for 2½ years;
- mention of new "challenges", such as climate change, to be faced by the European Union.

## Is the Lisbon Treaty merely a "resurrected" Constitutional Treaty?

There are differences between the two Treaties. The Constitutional Treaty was intended to provide an all-encompassing treaty whereas the Lisbon Treaty will only amend the existing Treaties. In addition, various controversial components of the Constitutional Treaty such as the promotion of a European motto and anthem, have been removed under the Lisbon Treaty. However, despite these and other differences, there is also a myriad of similarities between the two documents. For example, the removal of the pillar structure is integral to both Treaties, as is the elimination of the distinction between the EU and the EC. In addition, under both Treaties, the accession of the whole of the EU to the ECHR would have been assured.

### When will the Treaty of Lisbon become law?

The Treaty was expected to enter into force on 1 January 2009. However, this was subject to its ratification by all Member States. In June 2008, the Irish electorate voted "no" on the issue of ratification of the Treaty of Lisbon. As a consequence, the Treaty is not yet law. Most of the other Member States have, however, ratified the Treaty.

### Why did the Irish electorate reject the Treaty?

The reasons for the Irish rejection are complex and these will be examined in greater detail in the final chapter of this book. However, it is worth noting at this juncture that the issue of ratification is likely to be put to the Irish electorate again in 2009. At the time of writing, polls have suggested a rise in Irish support for the Treaty.

---

### Essential Facts

- It is impossible to understand the constitutional law of the European Union without first looking at the history of European integration.
- The end of the Second World War was a key point in the history of the development of the European Union.
- This history reflects the gradual widening of the European Community/European Union's competences to pass laws in an increasing number of areas.
- The extension of Europe's competence to more areas of law has not been uncontroversial. This is demonstrated by the recent rejection of the proposed Lisbon Treaty by the Irish electorate.
- The Treaty of Lisbon will not become law until all 27 Member States have ratified it.

## EUROPEAN INTEGRATION TIMELINE

| | |
|---|---|
| 1945: | End of the Second World War |
| May 1950: | Schuman Plan proposes the creation of the European Coal and Steel Community |
| April 1951: | Treaty establishing the European Coal and Steel Community signed |
| July 1952: | European Coal and Steel Community enters into force |
| March 1957: | Treaty establishing the European Economic Community and Treaty establishing the European Atomic Community signed in Rome |
| January 1958: | European Atomic Community and European Economic Community enter into force |
| April 1965: | Merger Treaty |
| January 1966: | Luxembourg Accords agreed |
| February 1986: | Single European Act signed |
| June 1987: | Single European Act enters into force |
| February 1992: | Treaty of Maastricht signed |
| November 1993: | Treaty of Maastricht comes into force, European Union an official entity |
| October 1997: | Treaty of Amsterdam signed |
| May 1999: | Treaty of Amsterdam comes into force |
| December 2000: | Treaty of Nice agreed |
| February 2003: | Treaty of Nice enters into force |
| July 2003: | Draft EU Constitution approved |
| May 2004: | Accession of 10 new Member States |
| November 2004: | EU Constitution signed |
| June 2007: | EU Constitution abandoned |
| December 2007: | Lisbon Treaty approved |
| June 2008: | Ireland votes "no" to Lisbon Treaty |
| June 2009: | European Parliamentary Elections |

# 2 MEMBERSHIP OF THE EUROPEAN UNION

## INTRODUCTION

The European Economic Community was founded in 1957 by six states: Germany, France, Belgium, the Netherlands, Italy and Luxembourg. Over time its membership has grown, so that a total of 27 countries are now members of the European Union. This chapter will detail the key stages in the enlargement of the Community before considering whether the Union is likely to expand beyond its existing membership.

## THE EVOLUTION FROM 6 TO 27 MEMBER STATES

The first enlargement of the Community occurred in 1973 with the entry of the United Kingdom, Ireland and the Netherlands. The United Kingdom made its first application for membership in 1961 but this was rejected as a result of the resistance of the French President, General de Gaulle, to the United Kingdom's accession. France was to go on to veto the United Kingdom's membership application on two separate occasions. The reason for General de Gaulle's rejection stemmed largely from a concern that the United Kingdom was too focused upon its relationship with the United States and the countries of the British Commonwealth. It was not until the resignation of General de Gaulle that the United Kingdom was able to accede to the Community along with Ireland and Denmark. At this point in time, Greenland was part of the Kingdom of Denmark, although in 1979 it obtained quasi-independence. It remained a member of the European Communities until its secession in 1985.

The next enlargement of the Community occurred in 1981 with the admission of Greece, followed in 1986 by the entry of Spain and Portugal. In 1990, the former (East) German Democratic Republic became a formal part of the Communities following the reunification of Germany. By 1995, the membership of the Union had increased to 15 states following the admission of Austria, Finland and Sweden. Norway had also been accepted to join in 1995 but did not accede following the results of a national referendum in which a majority of the Norwegian people voted against accession.

The biggest change to the membership of the European Union occurred in 2004 with the entry of Poland, the Czech Republic, Slovakia, Slovenia, Hungary, Malta, Cyprus, Latvia, Lithuania and Estonia to the

Union. This expansion was followed 3 years later with the addition of Bulgaria and Romania to the membership of the Union on 1 January 2007.

## Is membership of the Union likely to expand any further?

At present, three countries are formal candidates for membership of the European Union: Croatia, the former Yugoslav Republic of Macedonia and Turkey. However, negotiations with Turkey have been slow to progress and formal talks with Macedonia have yet to commence. Thus, of the three countries considered as official candidates for accession, Croatia is most likely to become the next member of the European Union.

Croatia's accession has to some extent been dependent upon its co-operation with the International Criminal Tribunal for the Former Yugoslavia based at The Hague. Indeed, formal accession talks were delayed until the UN Chief prosecutor at The Hague was able to confirm that the Croatian authorities were assisting in the investigation and prosecution of individuals responsible for war crimes in the early 1990s during the Serbo-Croatian war. At the time of writing, the target date for Croatia's entry is 2010/2011, although it is to be noted that Croatia's accession to the Union requires the consent of all Member States. Existing border tensions with Slovenia may hamper the path to membership.

A number of Western Balkan states such as Albania, Bosnia Herzegovina, Montenegro, Serbia and Kosovo have been promised membership of the European Union when they are able to fulfil the criteria for accession. At present, however, they are regarded as "potential candidate countries" and have not yet made official applications for membership. At the time of writing, it has also been reported that Iceland may make an application for membership, however no formal negotiations have yet been entered into.

## Which countries may apply to join the European Union?

Any European country which respects the principles set out in Arts 6 and 49 TEU may make an application for membership. In essence, this means that any European country which respects the principles of liberty, democracy, human rights and fundamental freedoms, and the rule of law may apply to become a member of the European Union.

There are several stages to the process of accession. First the country must make a formal application for membership. The application will then be reviewed by the Member States who will probably be assisted in this task by the Commission. Negotiations will commence if the existing Member States agree that the country should be considered as a "formal" candidate for membership. Negotiations are then broken down into several stages and involve ensuring that the candidate country is ready and indeed able to take on the obligations of membership. Once a country is in a position to accede, a Treaty of Accession will be drawn up. The country will only become a full member of the Union upon the ratification of the Treaty by all Member States. In addition, the Treaty will have to be ratified by the state wishing to accede to the Union. While this is usually a straightforward process, the failure by Norway to accede marks out that this can be a stumbling block to accession.

## What other criteria do candidate countries have to meet in order to join the European Union?

In 1993, a set of criteria called the "Copenhagen Criteria" was drawn up by the European Council. These are used to assess each applicant country's suitability for accession to the Union. The Copenhagen Criteria can be summarised as follows:

- A candidate country must be willing to accept *and* able to implement the entire corpus of European law as it has built up over time. This is referred to as the *acquis communautaire* and includes all the Treaties, Declarations, Protocols, secondary legislation, and agreements with third countries, Conventions and case law from the courts of the European Union.

- The applicant country must have a functioning market economy and be able to participate effectively within the internal market of the European Union. In addition, the candidate country should be able to meet the obligations of membership of the Union, particularly with regard to economic, political and monetary union.

- The candidate country must have stable institutions such as to guarantee democracy, respect for human rights and fundamental freedoms, and the rule of law and the protection of minorities.

In 1999 an additional "good neighbour" requirement was added to the criteria for entry. Essentially this requires all disputes with neighbouring states to be settled before a country will be allowed to accede to the Union. This was not possible in the case of Cyprus's accession in 2004, with the result that the Turkish part of the island did not join the EU.

The situation in Cyprus demonstrates that relations with the EU's neighbours are of paramount concern and, as a consequence, the European Commission in 2004 established a so-called European Neighbourhood Policy which aims to foster stronger links with countries to its south and east. The countries engaged by this policy are unlikely to become "formal" members of the EU but there is a growing realisation within European policy circles that internal stability is to some extent dependent upon good external relations. This is particularly true in areas such as energy co-operation, with certain parts of Europe increasingly dependent upon energy resources from Russia.

### Are there any conditions concerning the location of a candidate country?

Broadly speaking, a country must be "European" in order to accede to the European Union. While there is no definitive EU standard as to which countries are European, it is notable that in 1987 the Communities rejected an application for membership from Morocco on the ground that it was not European. However, this does not mean that non-European territories may never enjoy the benefits of Union membership (Art 299 EC). Thus the Portuguese islands of the Azores which are situated in the mid- Atlantic, as well as various Caribbean islands considered to be part of the Netherlands, are all covered by EU law.

### Once a country has been accepted as a member of the European Union, can it be expelled from the European Union?

There is no formal mechanism by which a Member State may be expelled from the Union. However, Art 7(1) and (2) of the Treaty on European Union sets out a procedure whereby a Member State may be censured and ultimately suspended from the Union in the event it fails to uphold the values of liberty, democracy, human rights and fundamental freedoms, and the rule of law upon which the Union is founded.

The procedure was first introduced by the Treaty of Amsterdam and was used in the late 1990s as a base upon which to impose unofficial and somewhat slapdash political sanctions against Austria following the formation of a coalition government which contained members from FPÖ, a far right political party. Following this incident, the procedure for censure and suspension was revised by the Treaty of Nice. The revisions aimed to introduce more by way of detail to the procedure so that it could be used in a more formal way and in a manner which gives the Member State concerned greater opportunities of defence. Interestingly, the Lisbon Treaty will, if adopted, establish a procedure under Art 50 TEU for the voluntary withdrawal of Member States from the Union. This is the first time such a provision has been explicitly provided for within any of the Treaties.

## CONCLUSION

The European Union of today is markedly different from the original political groupings which arose in Europe after the Second World War. The changes are most apparent in relation to the expansion of the European Union to 27 members. With Croatia likely to join in 2010/2011, membership will increase to 28 Member States. Given the scale of expansion which has been witnessed over the last decade, questions have been raised as to whether the EU should continue to expand. This theme will be explored further in Chapter 11.

### Essential Facts

- The European Union is currently composed of 27 Member States.
- Turkey, the Former Yugoslav Republic of Macedonia and Croatia are all "formal" candidates for accession to the European Union.
- Croatia is set to accede to the Union in 2010/2011.
- Candidates for membership are required to meet a set of criteria designed to ensure that they are ready for the obligations of membership.

# 3 THE EUROPEAN INSTITUTIONS

## INTRODUCTION

There are five main institutions outlined in Art 7 of the EC Treaty as being responsible for carrying out the functions of the Community. These are the Council, the Commission, the European Parliament, the European Court of Justice and the Court of Auditors. Each of these is responsible for ensuring the effective functioning and governance of the Community. In addition, there exist a number of other bodies responsible for the day-to-day operation of the Community. This chapter will look at the functions and composition of the following institutions:

- the European Council;
- the Council of the European Union;
- the European Commission;
- the European Parliament;
- the European Court of Justice;
- the Court of First Instance;
- the Court of Auditors.

### A caveat

While each of the institutions outlined above plays an important role in the "governance" of the Community, there is no "strict separation of powers" between each Community institution. Governance of the Community is therefore said to be *distributed*: *European Parliament v Council* (Case C 70/88) ("*Chernobyl*").

European governance may also be said to be *multi-level*, distributed between each of the European institutions and indeed the Member States themselves. This chapter will examine the composition and functions of the main European institutions but it should be borne in mind that this is merely a snapshot of the complex political and legal processes which combine to "run" Europe.

## THE EUROPEAN COUNCIL

### Composition

The European Council consists of Heads of State or Government of the Member States and the President of the Commission. It is assisted by the Foreign Ministers of the Member States and another member of the Commission. The European Council is a relatively new institution and was given formal recognition by the Single European Act (see Chapter 1). The role of the Council is now set out in Art 4 of the Treaty on European Union (TEU).

## Functions

The main role of the European Council is to represent the interests of the Member States at the highest political level. It is tasked to define the general guidelines of the Union and gives the necessary impetus for its development. The European Council usually meets around four times a year.

## Political role

The composition of the European Council means that it takes the major strategic decisions on the future development of the EU. It therefore helps to solve the "big", complicated political problems and at times acts as a forum for the mediation of disputes between Member States. The European Council also plays a crucial role in how the Union interacts with the outside world and is thus an important factor in the Union's external relations.

## THE COUNCIL OF THE EUROPEAN UNION (ARTS 202–210 EC)

### Composition

Pursuant to Art 203 EC, the Council of the European Union consists of one governmental representative at ministerial level for each Member State. It represents the interests of the governments of the Member States, with members acting in accordance with instructions received from their respective governments. It meets several times a month in either Brussels or Luxembourg.

In the past, the Council was referred to as the "Council of Ministers". However, it is now most commonly referred to simply as the "Council". For the purposes of simplicity, this text will therefore use the terminology "Council" when referring to the Council of the European Union.

### Which governmental Ministers are members of the Council of the European Union?

The membership of the Council is not fixed. Instead, it meets in nine different configurations depending upon the subject-matter being discussed. Meetings are attended by governmental Ministers responsible for the area concerned and there will always be as many members present as there are Member States. At present, there are nine such configurations:

- General Affairs and External Relations;
- Economic and Financial Affairs;
- Justice and Home Affairs;
- Employment, Social Policy, Health and Consumer Affairs;
- Competitiveness;
- Transport, Telecommunications and Energy;
- Agriculture and Fisheries;
- Environment;
- Education, Youth and Culture.

The existence of these different configurations necessitates the existence of a mechanism to ensure continuity, coherence and stability in the Council's work. A central role in providing such stability is played by the Committee of Permanent Representatives, usually known by the French acronym COREPER which is composed of permanent representatives from each of the Member States and is responsible for preparing and co-ordinating the work of the Council (Art 207(1) EC). COREPER is assisted in this task by a network of committees and working groups. The vast majority of decisions taken by the Council are in fact the product of work undertaken by COREPER. While further commentary is beyond the scope of this work, its influence upon the process of law making cannot be overestimated and has at times been controversial.

## Powers of the Council

### Legislative
The Council of the European Union plays a central role in the Union's legislative process.

- May request that the Commission generate legislative proposals (Art 208 EC).
- As part of its role in the legislative process, the Council on European Union votes on proposals which come from the Commission (Art 202 EC).
- It also authorises the Commission to negotiate international agreements (under Art 300 EC).

- The majority of legislative decisions made by the Council will be decided by something called "qualified majority voting". This is in essence a weighted system of voting, with voting power allocated on the basis of each country's population. The process was introduced to make the legislative process more responsive and efficient.

At the time of writing, the votes allocated to each Member State under the system of qualified majority are as follows:

> United Kingdom, Italy, Germany and France – 29 votes each
>
> Spain and Poland – 27 votes each
>
> Romania – 14 votes
>
> The Netherlands – 13 votes
>
> The Czech Republic, Greece, Hungary, Portugal, Belgium – 12 votes each
>
> Sweden, Austria and Bulgaria – 10 votes each
>
> Denmark, Lithuania, Ireland, Finland and Slovakia – 7 votes each
>
> Cyprus, Luxembourg, Slovenia, Latvia and Estonia – 4 votes each
>
> Malta – 3 votes.

A qualified majority is secured with 255 votes from a potential 345 (Art 205 EC).

- The system of qualified majority voting clearly gives states with larger populations more of a voice in the way in which decisions are made. However, at the same time, under this system individual Member States lose their power of veto over the enactment of legislation. The distribution of votes between Member States is thus a controversial area, with the consequence that some sensitive areas of Community competence still require the unanimous assent of Council members.

- The Council is also the principal institution responsible for law making in relation to Common Foreign and Security Policy and Police and Judicial Co-operation in Criminal Matters.

### Budgetary and economic

The Council has competence over certain budgetary and economic matters:

- together with the Parliament, the Council drafts and adopts the budget for the EC (Art 272 EC);
- under Art 202 EC, the Council is required to "ensure effective co-ordination of the general economic policies of the Member States".

*Executive/administrative*

The Council exercises the following executive power:

- its capacity to ensure co-ordination of the general economic policies of the Member States (Art 99 EC).

## The role of the Council Presidency

An important role is played by the Council "President". This is rotated among Member States every 6 months on a predetermined basis in accordance with the procedure outlined in Art 203 EC.

The Council Presidency is not merely an honorary role. Instead, the Member State holding the Presidency performs a number of important functions in relation to the governance of the Union. The most important of these functions can be summarised as follows:

- responsible for chairing all Council and working group meetings;
- represents the Council in its dealings with the other EU institutions;
- tasked to represent the EU as a whole when negotiating with external institutions and non-EU states.

If the Treaty of Lisbon enters into force, the role of the Council President will change. Instead of being rotated on a 6-monthly basis, the position will be held for 2½ years and this term will be renewable.

## A point of note

Unfortunately, there are rather a lot of Councils in European legal circles. In addition to the two councils which exist as institutions of the European Union, there is also the Council of Europe, an intergovernmental body which is responsible for a variety of tasks, the best known of which is administering the European Convention on Human Rights. The Council of Europe enjoys a much bigger membership than the European Union, with 47 states as contracting parties. With all these Councils involved in European public affairs, it is important not to get mixed up between them.

## THE EUROPEAN COMMISSION (ARTS 211–219 EC)

### Composition

Members of the European Commission are called "Commissioners". At present, there are 27 Commissioners, one for each Member State.

However, the recent enlargement of the European Union led to an agreement between the Member States that there should no longer be one Commissioner for every member.

The Treaty of Lisbon provides that from 1 November 2014, the number of Commissioners will correspond to two-thirds of the number of Member States. In addition to the Commissioners, this number will include the Commission President and High Representative of the Union for Foreign Affairs and Security Policy. This number may be changed should the European Council, acting unanimously, decide upon an amendment. In this regard, it seems likely that, as a concession to Ireland, following its rejection of the Treaty of Lisbon, a decision will be taken which will retain the existing status quo such that there will be one Commissioner for each Member State. However, there are concerns that a Commission comprising such a large number of Commissioners may be too large and unwieldy.

The present roster of Commissioners entered office in November 2004 and is tasked to serve a 5-year term. The next Commission will thus be appointed in November 2009. Commission terms of office coincide with the period in relation to which the European Parliament is elected.

## Representation

Commissioners represent the interests of the Union as a whole and are tasked under Art 213 EC to be independent of national interests and instead consider the "Community interest" when making decisions.

## Appointment and removal

The method for appointing Commissioners is set out in Art 214 EC. This outlines that the Council, meeting as Heads of State and acting by a qualified majority, is responsible for nominating the person it intends to appoint to be the President of the Commission. This nomination is then put to the European Parliament for approval. The process for appointing individual Commissioners is similar and commences with each Member State tabling proposals for potential Commissioners. The Council, working with the nominee for President and acting by a qualified majority, then draws up a list of individuals whom it intends to appoint as Commissioners. This list is then subject to approval by the European Parliament.

With regard to the removal of individual Commissioners from their posts, Art 216 EC provides that the Council or Commission may make an application to the European Court of Justice to bring about such a removal if the Commissioner in question "no longer fulfils the conditions required for the performance of his duties or if he has been guilty of serious misconduct". In the past, individual Commissioners have been the subject of allegations of fraud and misconduct. In 1999, the so-called Santer Commission (named after its President) resigned *en masse* after an investigation by the Court of Auditors and the European Parliament found evidence of financial impropriety. As a result of issues surrounding the resignation of the Santer Commission, it was decided that a more effective way of dismissing individual Commissioners was required. The Treaty of Nice therefore introduced a Treaty amendment so that Art 217(4) EC now provides for the compulsory resignation of a Commissioner upon the request of the President of the Commission and approval of the rest of the Commissioners.

## Organisation

The work of the Commission is organised into a variety of subsections called Directorates General (DGs). There are 40 such DGs, each with competence over a particular area of policy making. In relation, every Commissioner has competence over at least one policy area and so the head of each DG will ultimately be responsible to the relevant Commissioner for that area. The work of the Commission is assisted by around 24,000 permanent members of staff.

## The role of the Commission President

The importance accorded to the position of Commission President has increased greatly of late. Pursuant to Art 217 EC, the Commission is required to work under the "political guidance" of its President. The President is also responsible for allocating policy areas to each individual Commissioner and, as outlined above, plays an important role in relation to the removal of Commissioners.

## Powers

### Legislative

The Commission plays a central role in the making of legislation:

- The Commission proposes EC legislation to the Council and the European Parliament (Art 211 EC). The Commission is therefore said to have the "right of initiative" over EC legislation and thus plays a significant role in setting the legislative agenda of the EC.

*Executive/administrative*

- The Commission is called the "guardian of the Treaties". This refers
  to the powers of the Commission to ensure the proper implementation of Community law. These powers allow the Commission to
  bring infringement proceedings against Member States before the
  European Court of Justice for failure to fulfil an obligation under
  Community law. This power is set down in Art 226 EC.

## THE EUROPEAN PARLIAMENT (ARTS 189–201 EC)

### Composition

In the founding Treaties, the Parliament was originally referred to as
the "Assembly" and consisted of representatives appointed by national
Parliaments. In 1962, the members of the Assembly opted to change the
institution's name to the European Parliament.

Since 1979, members of the Parliament have been directly elected
by the peoples of Europe. Indeed, the Parliament is currently the only
directly elected institution of the European Union. All citizens of the
European Union are entitled to vote and stand in these elections which
are held every 5 years. The next set of parliamentary elections will take
place in June 2009.

The maximum number of Members of the European Parliament is
required under Art 189 EC not to exceed 739. However, as an interim
measure following the recent enlargement of the Union, there are at
present 785 Members of the European Parliament (MEPs). Seats are
apportioned among Member States, with no country allowed more than
99 seats or fewer than 5. The number of MEPs will decrease to 736
with the commencement of the next parliamentary term. However, the
number of MEPs will increase to 751 upon the ratification of the Lisbon
Treaty. In addition, under the Treaty no Member State will be permitted
to have more than 96 or fewer than 6 MEPs.

Members of the European Parliament are organised in cross-national
political groups which span a wide range of political views. At present,
there are seven such groupings as well as a cluster of "non-aligned" MEPs.
The Parliament's Rules of Procedure set out a number of criteria which
must be met before a "new" political grouping can come into existence,
including a condition relating to the minimum number of MEPs within
any one group. This is in part a strategy to prevent small groups with
extreme political views establishing a foothold within the European
Parliament.

At present, the political groupings within the European Parliament are as follows:

* Group of the European People's Party (Christian Democrats) and European Democrats;
* Socialist group;
* Group of the Alliance of Liberals and Democrats for Europe;
* Union for Europe of the Nations Group;
* Group of the Greens/European Free Alliance;
* Confederal Group of the European United Left – Nordic Green Left;
* Independence/Democracy Group.

These groupings are recognised under Art 191 EC as contributing to the formation of a European political awareness and, as such, "to expressing the political will of the citizens of the Union". However, this description largely ignores the fact that voter turnout in European parliamentary elections is traditionally extremely low. In recognition of this, various strategies have been put in place to promote better engagement between voters and their elected officials.

## Powers

The powers enjoyed by the Parliament have improved considerably in the last few years. This is particularly true in the legislative sphere, with the Parliament increasingly taking on the role of an equal partner in the making of legislation.

### Legislative

* The Parliament adopts legislation jointly with the Council under the co-decision procedure (Art 251 EC). This procedure has become an increasingly common way of law making in the Community. If the Treaty of Lisbon is passed into law, the co-decision procedure will be renamed the "ordinary procedure", reflecting its use as the most common way of making law in the EC.
* Not all laws are passed using the co-decision procedure and so the involvement of the European Parliament in the law-making process varies. Areas which are politically sensitive will generally utilise special legislative procedures which do not grant the Parliament an equal role in the law-making process. More detail on this is provided in Chapter 5.

- The Parliament may also request that the Commission submit legislative proposals and so has some power of legislative initiative (Art 192(2) EC).
- It approves certain international agreements concluded by the Council (Art 300(3) EC).

## Budgetary

- Together with the Council, the Parliament approves the EC budget (Art 272 EC).

## Powers of review

- The Parliament enjoys the competence to dismiss the entire Commission (Art 201 EC).
- The Parliament approves the President and other members of the Commission (Art 214(2) EC).
- It has the capacity to investigate breaches or maladministration in relation to the implementation of EC law (Art 193 EC).
- It has "standing" to challenge the legality of Community legislation in front of the ECJ (Art 230 EC).
- It performs a supervisory role in relation to the Council. To this end, it issues reports three times a year on the activities of the Council.

## What other supervisory powers does the Parliament have which might be of assistance to individual European citizens?

- The Parliament receives petitions by EU citizens or Member State residents on matters within Community competence directly affecting them (Art 194 EC).
- It elects and appoints the European Ombudsman, which investigates citizens' complaints regarding the activities of the EC institutions (Art 195 EC).

## THE EUROPEAN COURT OF JUSTICE (ECJ) (ARTS 220–245 EC)

### Origins and development of the European Court of Justice

The origins of the European Court of Justice go back to 1951 with the formation of the European Coal and Steel Community (ECSC). The Treaty which formed the ECSC explicitly provided for the formation of a "Court of Justice" to ensure the proper interpretation and application of the Treaty. A Court of Justice was also provided for under the 1957 Treaties establishing the European Economic Community and the European Atomic Energy Community. In order to avoid unnecessary duplication of institutional competences between each of the newly created European Communities, it was decided that on the coming into force of Euratom and the EEC in 1958, there would exist only one "Court of Justice". This decision thereby marked the establishment of the European Court of Justice. Under the Treaty of Lisbon, the European Court of Justice will be renamed the "Court of Justice of the European Union".

## Composition and appointment

The European Court of Justice is composed of 27 judges and eight Advocates General. All judges and Advocates General are appointed by common agreement among the Governments of the Member States. Under Art 221 EC, there is one judge per Member State. In relation to appointment of Advocates General, the practice has been for each of the five largest Member States to put forward one nomination, with the remaining positions assigned among the other Member States on a rotational basis. The initial period of office applicable to the appointment of both judges and Advocates General is 6 years, although this may be renewed.

The independence of judges and Advocates General to the European Court of Justice must be beyond doubt. In addition, they are required to possess the qualifications required for appointment, in their Member State, to the highest judicial offices, or be jurists of recognised competence (Arts 221–223 EC).

## The role of the Advocate General

Article 222 EC states the role of the Advocate General:

> "It shall be the duty of the Advocate General, acting with complete impartiality and independence, to make, in open court, reasoned submissions on cases which, in accordance with the Statute of the Court of Justice, require his involvement."

The role of the Advocate General is therefore to provide a reasoned opinion on certain matters before the European Court of Justice at the oral stage of judicial proceedings. The opinion issued by the Advocate

General is then submitted to the European Court of Justice. While the opinion of the Advocate General is not strictly binding, the Court may take it into account. Indeed, given the collegiate style of ECJ judgments (see below), the opinion of the Advocate General is often much easier to read and is usually influential upon the Court's final decision.

## Jurisdiction of the European Court of Justice

Article 220 EC tasks the ECJ to ensure that the law is observed. In addition to this, Arts 226–243 EC set out the primary factual jurisdiction of the Court. This can be summarised as follows:

- power to consider whether a Member State has failed to fulfil an obligation under the EC Treaty (Arts 226 and 227 EC);
- may impose penalties upon Member States for failure to fulfil a Community law obligation (Art 228 EC);
- competence to review the legality of an act of the Community as well as to declare it void (Arts 230 and 231 EC);
- power to review an action against the main Community institutions for failure to act (Art 232 EC);
- competence to receive preliminary ruling requests from national courts (Art 234 EC);
- power to act as an appellate court in relation to judgments issued by the CFI (Art 225 EC);
- power under Art 300(6) EC to issue a binding opinion on whether an agreement concluded between the Community and one or more states or with an international organisation is compatible with Community law (exercised upon the request of the European Parliament, the Council, the Commissioner or a Member State).

## Organisation of the European Court of Justice

When hearing a case, the European Court of Justice can sit either as a full Court or in smaller sub-groups called Chambers. The composition of the Court will very much depend upon the case being heard, although, as a general rule of thumb, it can be stated that the more important a case, the greater the number of judges who will be involved in it.

## The "form" of ECJ judgments

Judgments issued by the ECJ tend to differ from those given by higher courts in the UK. One significant difference is that ECJ judgments are collegiate and so are constructed as a single ruling, with no dissenting judgments published. In the event that there is a disagreement among the judges involved in the case, a vote will be taken and the decision of the majority will decide the result of the case. This does not always bode well for the clarity of ECJ judgments.

## The doctrine of precedent and ECJ judgments

The doctrine of *stare decisis* means to stand by one's decisions. *Stare decisis* is another way of stating that the doctrine of precedent applies to a court's decisions. While the European Court of Justice does tend to follow its own previous rulings, it is not strictly bound to do so and so the doctrine of *stare decisis* does not apply.

## Criticisms of the European Court of Justice

As will be exemplified in the following chapters, the Court has been at the forefront of the process of European integration. During periods of political stagnation, the judgments of the Court have helped to ensure the continued development of the European political "project". As a consequence of such dynamism, the Court has faced a myriad of criticism that it has been rather too active. This has led to the portrayal by Euro-sceptics [people critical of European integration] of judges of the ECJ as akin to "politicians in robes". Whether such criticisms are deserved is a question beyond the scope of this work. However, what is undeniable is the impact of the judgments of the ECJ upon the legal map of Europe.

The impact of the ECJ is arguably a consequence of its "success" in attracting cases. From a slow trickle of cases in the early 1960s, the ECJ now considers thousands of cases a year. The increasing workload of the Court led to the creation of the Court of First Instance which was intended to reduce the burden upon the ECJ.

## THE COURT OF FIRST INSTANCE (CFI)

There are currently 27 judges appointed to the Court of First Instance – one for each Member State. No Advocates General are appointed to the Court of First Instance, although, in exceptional circumstances, this task may be fulfilled by a judge. Judges are appointed for a period of 6 years upon the joint agreement of all Member States. Their term of office is renewable. As in the European Court of Justice, the independence and competence of judges to the Court of First Instance must be beyond doubt.

The Court of First Instance was created in 1988 and, as indicated, was intended to help reduce the workload of the European Court of Justice. Initially, however, the Court of First Instance was quite restricted in the types of case it could hear. Its jurisdiction has increased in recent years, although there are still jurisdictional differences between the two courts. In addition, Court of First Instance rulings are subject to appeal on points of law before the ECJ. Under the Treaty of Lisbon, the Court of First Instance is renamed the "General Court".

## Jurisdiction of the Court of First Instance

Pursuant to Art 225 EC, the Court of First Instance has jurisdiction to hear the following types of case:

- judicial review of an act of the Community institutions (in accordance with the procedure set out under Art 230 EC);
- failure of one of the Community institutions to act (under Art 232 EC);
- certain types of preliminary ruling request (under Art 234 EC and as defined by statute);
- an action for damages relating to the non-contractual liability of the Community (Art 235 EC);
- disputes relating to Staff Regulations and Conditions of Employment arising between the Community and its servants (Art 237 EC).

## Judicial panels

The Treaty of Nice provides for the establishment of so-called judicial panels so as to lessen the burden upon the CFI. Members are appointed by the Council acting under unanimity. Decisions of judicial panels are subject to appeal to the CFI.

## COURT OF AUDITORS

The Court of Auditors was established in 1975 under the Budgetary Treaty. It name reflects its main institutional role which is to audit the budget of the European Communities. It currently has 27 members – one for each Member State.

## WHO IS IN CHARGE?

It was noted at the beginning of this chapter that governance of the European Union is multi-level and distributed among the different institutions and the Member States. It is therefore important to remember that, as a result of this diffusion of competences, no one institution is in charge of the governance of Europe. Accordingly, there is no one legislative, executive or judicial branch. Theories of governance applicable to the domestic sphere do not therefore provide a particularly useful lens through which to study the way in which the EU of today is governed.

Various theories of European governance abound and it is beyond the scope of this work to examine these in any great detail. However, of late, there has been a move away from "old" forms of governance which involve "top down" hierarchical decision making towards the development of "new" governance models based upon flexibility and inclusivity. As such, the preceding exposition of the main European institutions should be approached with the caveat that new forms of governance are being developed which include a variety of actors.

### Essential Facts

- The European Council is composed of the Heads of State or government of each Member State. It represents the interests of Member States at the highest level.
- The Council of the European Union is composed of governmental representatives at ministerial level and represents the interests of the Member States.
- The Commission represents the interests of the EU as a whole and is independent of national governments.
- The European Parliament is directly elected by EU citizens and is responsible for representing their interests.
- The European Court of Justice and the Court of First Instance are tasked to ensure the observance of Community law.

# 4 SOURCES OF COMMUNITY LAW

This chapter will examine the main sources of Community law. It is to be noted that the title of this chapter refers to "Community law", and not "European Union law". The distinction made here is not merely one of semantics. Rather, the focus of this chapter will be upon the sources of law and legislative processes applicable to the first pillar.

The main sources of Community law are as follows.

## PRIMARY SOURCES OF COMMUNITY LAW

The most important sources of Community law are the Treaties establishing the three European Communities: the EC Treaty, the ECSC Treaty (which from 2002 is no longer in force) and the Treaty establishing the European Atomic Energy Community. The provisions of each of these Treaties have been added to and amended over time, with the most significant changes emanating from the amendments introduced by the Single European Act, the Treaty on European Union (TEU), the Treaty of Amsterdam and the Treaty of Nice. Modifications have also been introduced to the "original" Treaties as a result of the accession of new Member States and the addition of various "protocols" annexed to the main text of both the EC Treaty and the TEU.

If the Treaty of Lisbon enters into force, two Treaties will exist: an amended TEU and a Treaty on the Functioning of the European Union (TFEU) which will replace the EC Treaty.

## The EC Treaty

The EC Treaty represents only a small fragment of the law of the Community as it exists today. The significance of the EC Treaty is that it sets out the goals of the Community and also its competence to enact secondary legislation to achieve these goals. At the time of their formation, the Communities were focused upon the achievement of economic objectives; these goals have changed markedly and now reflect aims such as "balanced and sustainable development" as well as a "high level of protection and improvement of the quality of the environment".

While the EC Treaty represents the "bare bones" of Community law, this is not to say that it does not contain important sources of law.

Rather, these are complemented by a roster of secondary legislation, case law, international agreements, and general principles of law together with other, non-binding, sources of law. We will deal with each of these sources in turn.

## GENERAL PRINCIPLES OF EC LAW

The ECJ has extracted a series of general principles from the legal system of the Member States which it uses as an aid to both interpretation and review of Community law and the actions of Member States. Various principles of law have been found to be applicable to the Community legal system, including those of proportionality, non-discrimination, legal certainty and equality.

As an aid to interpretation, the general principles have performed an important "gap filling" mechanism applicable in the event of an omission either in the Treaties or under secondary legislation. Breach of one of the general principles of Community law also provides a fertile ground for judicial review both of the acts of the Community as well as of certain acts of the Member States. The general principles may also be utilised in the review of certain acts of the Member States.

### Fundamental human rights

An important development in the jurisprudence of Community law has been the recognition given by the Court to the importance of protecting fundamental human rights. Such protections are regarded as general principles of Community law and so the Community courts are tasked to ensure their observance.

An important judgment on the development of fundamental human rights as part of the general principles of community law is that of *Internationale Handelsgesellschaft und Vorratsstelle Getreide* (Case 11/70). It centred upon concerns that specific provisions of Community law were contrary to fundamental rights protections set out in the German constitution. The case is dealt with in more detail in Chapter 6 on supremacy, for in its judgment the ECJ found that Community law has primacy over conflicting national law, even that emanating from national constitutions. For those concerned that the primacy of Community law could result in erosion of fundamental rights protections guaranteed by national constitutional traditions, the ECJ responded that fundamental rights are in fact part of Community law. Accordingly, the Court held that:

"[R]espect for fundamental rights forms an integral part of the general principles protected by the Court of Justice. The protection of such rights, whilst inspired by the constitutional traditions common to the Member States, must be ensured within the framework of the structure and objectives of the Community."

Since its decision in *Internationale Handelsgesellschaft*, the ECJ has issued a series of judgments elucidating upon the nature of fundamental rights protections within the Community legal order. Central to the development of such protections has been the recognition given by the European Court of Justice to the relevance of the European Convention on Human Rights (ECHR) as a source of inspiration in the interpretation of Community law. This recognition is evident in *Nold* (Case 4/73) in which the European Court of Justice outlined that the ECHR "can supply guidelines which should be followed within the framework of Community law". In this regard, it is important to note that the European Court of Human Rights has recently held that the system of fundamental rights protection existent within the EU is currently "equivalent" to that available under the ECHR, although this could potentially be subject to change: *Bosphorus v Ireland* (Application No 45036/98).

At the same time, the Community institutions have incorporated references to fundamental human rights into the Treaties. Of great significance is Art 6(2) TEU which enacts that the Union is founded upon respect for human rights and fundamental freedoms as well as the principles of liberty and democracy. If the Lisbon Treaty is adopted, the Union as a whole will accede to the European Convention on Human Rights (ECHR). However, whether this will have a significant impact upon the protection afforded to fundamental rights within the Union is debatable.

## SECONDARY SOURCES OF COMMUNITY LAW

So as to enable it to carry out the tasks specified in the Treaty, the Community and its institutions are authorised to enact secondary legislation. This competence is set out in Art 249 EC, which provides:

"In order to carry out their task and in accordance with the provisions of this Treaty, the European Parliament acting jointly with the Council and the Commission shall make regulations and issue directives, take decisions, make recommendations or deliver opinions."

We shall deal with each of these secondary sources of Community law in turn.

## Regulations

A Regulation, as defined in Art 249 EC, shall "have general application. It shall be binding in its entirety and directly applicable in all Member States". The meaning of each of these phrases is as follows:

- Regulations have "general application". This means that they are not addressed to specific individuals but instead "produce legal effects with regard to persons described in a generalised and abstract manner": *Koninklijke Scholten Honing* v *Council and Commission* (Case 101/76).

- Regulations are "binding in [their] entirety". This means that introduction of any national legislation which affects the content of a Regulation is prohibited. As a consequence, Member States are required to refrain from adopting any implementing measures: *Variola SpA* v *Amministrazione delle Finanze* (Case 34/73).

- Regulations are "directly applicable". As a consequence, they automatically become part of the domestic law of Member States without any national implementing legislation being required: *Leonesio* v *Ministry for Agriculture* (Case 93/71).

- Regulations are required to be published in a document called the *Official Journal*. This acts as a repository for all official publications of the European Union. They enter into force either on the date specified within the Regulation itself or 20 days after publication in the *Official Journal*.

Regulations are a good way of ensuring the uniform application of Community law. To this end, under a recent programme of legislative reform instituted by the Community, an increased emphasis has been placed upon the use of Regulations as opposed to Directives, to ensure that such uniformity is achieved.

## Directives

Directives are noted by Art 249 EC to be "binding as to the result to be achieved, upon each Member State to which [they are] addressed, but shall leave to the national authorities the choice of form and methods". The following points may be made as to the legal effect of a Directive:

- Directives are not necessarily addressed to all Member States. As a consequence, they are binding only upon the Member State(s) to whom they are addressed.

- The Member States addressed in a Directive are required to implement its provisions into their own national law. While the choice of form and methods for implementation will be within the discretion of the Member State, the aim specified in the Directive must be achieved.

- A Directive will normally specify a time limit for implementation. If no date is specified, the Directive will enter into force 20 days after publication. The overwhelming majority of Directives are required to be published in the *Official Journal* (Art 254 EC).

Directives are useful legislative instruments as, unlike Regulations, they offer Member States flexibility with regard to how to implement their obligations under Community law.

## Decisions

- Article 249 notes that a "decision shall be binding in its entirety upon those to whom it is addressed".

- Decisions may be thought of as mini-Regulations. They do not require national implementing measures and enter into force automatically. However, unlike Regulations, which are addressed to all Member States, Decisions are addressed to specific persons or Member States. They may even be addressed to companies.

- Most decisions are required to be published in the *Official Journal* (Art 254 EC). They enter into force either on the date specified within the Decision itself or 20 days after publication in the *Official Journal*.

## Who decides which legislative instrument to use?

Before Community legislation may be enacted, it must have a legislative base. Accordingly, under Art 253 EC, when the Community enacts secondary legislation in the form of Regulations, Directives and Decisions, a statement should be made as to the legal base upon which the legislation is made.

The choice of which legislative form to use is dependent upon the legislative base used to justify enactment of the measure in question. Where no legislative form is specified, the choice of which instrument to use will be left to the Community institutions involved. However, the decision as to the legislative base used is open to examination by the Community courts.

## Recommendations and opinions

These are noted in Art 249 EC as having no binding force. However, this does not mean that they cannot produce legal effects and, as such, they may have persuasive force: *Grimaldi* v *Fonds des Maladies Professionnelles* (Case C-322/88). Recommendations and opinions are a form of soft law.

## Soft law

The term "soft law" is used to refer to legislation which is not binding. The Community institutions have developed various soft law instruments to achieve the aims set out in the Treaties. The advantage of such instruments is that, as non-binding sources of law, they offer much-needed flexibility to achieving the aims of the Community.

## INTERNATIONAL AGREEMENTS

Under Art 300(7) EC, international agreements entered into by the Community with third countries or other international organisations are important components of Community law and are hence binding upon Community institutions: *Haegeman* v *Belgium* (Case 181/73).

## THE INFLUENCE OF THE CASE LAW OF THE ECJ AND CFI

As will be demonstrated in the following chapters, the development by the ECJ of principles such as direct effect, supremacy and state liability has had a profound impact upon the development of Community law. While the judgments of the Community courts are not formal sources of law, they are included here as a reflection of their influence upon the Community legal order.

## THE RECEPTION OF THE SOURCES OF COMMUNITY LAW INTO THE UK

The obligation of Member States to abide by Community law is outlined in Art 10 EC which notes that they are required to take "all appropriate measures, whether general or particular, to ensure fulfilment of the obligations arising out of this Treaty or resulting from action taken by the institutions of the Community ... They shall abstain from any measure which could jeopardise the attainment of the objectives of the Community".

The UK adopts a so-called "dualist" slant with regard to international law. This means that it does not consider international law to be part of its domestic law unless and until it has been incorporated by means of an Act of Parliament. The legal system established by the Community was incorporated into UK law by means of the European Communities Act 1972. More consideration will be given to this in Chapter 6 on the doctrine of supremacy.

## Essential Facts

- Community law has numerous sources, the most important of which are the provisions of the EC Treaty.

- The EC Treaty has been added to and amended many times and it is clear that both the aim and the scope of the original EEC Treaty have expanded considerably over the years.

- Secondary legislation is also a major source of Community law. The competence of the Community to enact such legislation is found in the Treaties.

- The main forms of secondary legislation are Directives, Decisions and Regulations.

- International agreements are also important sources of Community law.

- The judgments of the Court of First Instance and the European Court of Justice, while not formal sources of law, have been incredibly influential on the subsequent development of the Community.

# 5 COMMUNITY LAW MAKING

The previous chapter set out the main sources of Community law. Of particular note are the various forms of secondary legislation that may be enacted by the Community institutions. This chapter will now go on to examine how law is made within the Community, with a particular emphasis being laid upon the processes involved in the formulation of secondary legislation.

## LIMITED POWERS

Law making within the Community is subject to the doctrine of "limited powers". This is set out in Art 5 EC which provides:

> "The Community shall act within the limits of the powers conferred upon it by this Treaty and of the objectives assigned to it therein."

What this means is that the Community must act within the limits of its powers when enacting legislation. The powers of the Community are outlined in the Treaties so, in practice, this requires there to be a legal base within the Treaties. As noted in the previous chapter, Art 253 EC requires a statement to be made as to the legal base used to enact secondary legislation.

## THE CHOICE OF A LEGAL BASE

The choice of legal base used to enact legislation will very much depend upon the aim or purpose of the proposed legislation. The choice of legal base will have consequences for the legislative procedure actually used to enact legislation. This is because if a law is enacted pursuant to a particular Treaty Article, the Article *itself* may require a specific legislative process to be utilised. This will have ramifications for the institutional actors involved in the decision-making process. As a consequence, the choice of legal base may be subject to "judicial review" by the Court under the process summarised in Art 230 EC. As outlined by the European Court in *Commission* v *Council (Generalised Tariff Preferences)* (Case 45/86):

> "(T)he choice of the legal basis for a measure may not depend simply on an institution's conviction as to the objective pursued but must be based on objective factors which are amenable to judicial review."

## LEGISLATIVE PROCEDURES

The main procedures through which the European institutions adopt legislation under the first pillar are detailed below. These processes have emerged over time and have become increasingly complex. The Lisbon Treaty, if adopted, will streamline the way in which European law is made. Where relevant, mention will be made of the changes which will be brought about by the new Treaty.

There are currently four main processes through which secondary legislation in the Community is adopted:

- co-decision procedure;
- assent procedure;
- co-operation procedure;
- consultation procedure;

Each of these procedures involves the interaction of the Commission, the Council and the European Parliament to a greater or lesser degree. The process of law making in the Community usually commences with the Commission, which enjoys the right of legislative initiative over Community legislation. To assist the Commission in identifying areas which may require legislation, both the Parliament (under Art 192(2) EC) and the Council (under Art 208 EC) may make legislative proposals to it.

### Co-decision procedure (Art 251 EC)

The most important legislative procedure for the enactment of Community law is the process outlined in Art 251 EC. This procedure, termed "co-decision", was introduced by the TEU and was designed to provide the Parliament with the authority to suggest amendments to proposed legislation. Changes were made to the procedure by the Treaty of Amsterdam, with the consequence that the Parliament now has a much more equal role in this legislative procedure. Formerly, under the procedure introduced by the TEU, the Council could by unanimity revert to its original common position in the event that it disagreed with the suggestions put forward by the Parliament; the post-Amsterdam co-decision procedure precludes this. The use of co-decision was further extended by the Treaty of Nice, such that the procedure is now used in the majority of areas of Community competence. If the Treaty of Lisbon is adopted, co-decision will become the "norm" and will be renamed the "ordinary legislative procedure". Increased use of the co-decision procedure allows for more democratic decision making given the role played by the Parliament which is directly elected by EU citizens.

## Assent procedure (Art 250 EC)

The assent procedure was introduced by the Single European Act and requires the *positive* assent of the Parliament before legislation may be adopted by the Council. Under this procedure, the Parliament is granted considerable power over the law-making process. It is employed in a number of different areas such as the acceptance of new Member States to the EU (Art 49 TEU) and in the procedure for sanctioning Member States under Art 7(?) TEU (see commentary in Chapter 2).

## Co-operation procedure (Art 252 EC)

This procedure was introduced by the Single European Act and was intended to enhance the role of the Parliament in the law-making process. It grants the Parliament two readings of proposed legislation but does not give it a veto. The use of the co-operation procedure has declined in recent years as a consequence of the increased use of co-decision. Following changes introduced by the Treaty of Nice, very few Treaty Articles require the use of the co-operation procedure.

## Consultation procedure

This procedure involves the Council and Commission acting together to make legislation. While the Parliament has the right to be consulted, its opinion may be disregarded and the legislation adopted anyway. Under this process, the Parliament hence has no real power over the enactment of legislation. The procedure is used to enact legislation in a number of politically sensitive areas such as agricultural policy.

## THEMES WHICH HAVE EMERGED OVER TIME IN THE LEGISLATIVE PROCESS

The legislative procedures outlined above are the product of recent efforts to enhance the involvement of the Parliament in the law-making process. This is in part a response to concerns surrounding the lack of democratic accountability within the European law-making process. Since the Parliament is the only directly elected institution within the Community, promoting its position within the legislative process is therefore an important element in "democratising" the Community.

However, despite increased involvement of the Parliament, the process of law making is far from straightforward, with the result that citizens tend to feel quite disconnected from it. This is in part a response to the overtly complex and bureaucratic nature of the law-making process. To this end, an additional trend associated with the law-making process within the Community has been the significant effort exerted by the Community to reduce the bureaucracy associated with the process of enacting legislation. So the Commission is increasingly shying away from the use of traditional, "top-down" legislative instruments and, instead, exploring new forms of governance which place an emphasis upon the value of "soft" rather than hard law. The existence of "new governance" processes belies a concern that the existing legislative processes and instruments are too bureaucratic and are in danger of distancing the Union even further from its citizens.

The Community institutions have therefore committed themselves to a programme focused upon "Better Regulation". This is designed to simplify and streamline European legislation. As part of this process, the Commission has commenced a review of existing legislation and is slowly removing obsolete and irrelevant provisions. It has also placed a premium upon the use of "co-regulation" and self-regulation. These forms of law making are very much reliant upon the involvement of non-state actors such as industry bodies and other interest groups.

Thus the above description of the law-making processes within the European Community does not provide the whole picture. It should rather be thought of as a snapshot of how the Community institutions interact to generate certain forms of legislation.

## Essential Facts

- There are currently four main procedures through which law is made in the European Community:
    - consultation procedure;
    - co-operation procedure;
    - co-decision procedure;
    - assent procedure.
- Each of these procedures involves the interaction of the Parliament, Commission and the Council, although the involvement of each varies according to the process used.

- The process by which legislation is made within the Community has not been static and, over time, the involvement of each institutional actor has changed.
- The involvement of the European Parliament in the legislative process has increased markedly of late, particularly through the introduction of the co-decision procedure.
- If the Treaty of Lisbon is adopted, the co-decision procedure will be renamed the "ordinary legislative procedure".
- There has also been a trend towards utilising less formal legislative styles in order to bring the process of law making "closer" to European citizens. To this end, the use of soft law is being promoted.

# 6 SUPREMACY

## THE DOCTRINE OF SUPREMACY

Since the inception of the Treaty of Rome in 1957, questions have been raised concerning the effect of Community law upon national law. In the event of a conflict between a provision of Community law and a national law, which one should take precedence? In essence, which source of law has "supremacy" over the other? Unfortunately, no definitive statement on the primacy of European law over conflicting national law was provided within the original Treaties. However, various "signposts" were provided which alluded to the nature of the relationship between Community and domestic law. Thus, under Art 249 EC, Regulations were noted to be "directly applicable", while, under Art 292 EC, a direction is made such that, in the event of a disagreement concerning the interpretation or implementation of Community law, recourse is to be had only to Community dispute settlement methods. In addition, under what is now Art 10 EC, Member States are under a duty to refrain from adopting measures which would compromise the attainment of the objectives of the Treaty.

It is likely that the omission of a precise statement on the primacy of Community law over national law was not merely an oversight. Instead, the failure is probably the result of diplomatic concerns. An official pronouncement in the original founding Treaties on the "supremacy" of European law may have resulted in the withdrawal of certain Member States from membership of the Community. This resulted in the European Court of Justice being left to "fill in the gaps".

The European Court of Justice approached this task in an incremental fashion, issuing a series of judgments which established that the law of the European Community *should* have supremacy over conflicting national law. We shall deal with each of these judgments in turn, examining the reasoning of the Court for establishing the doctrine of the supremacy of Community law and detailing the impact of the doctrine in the UK. A caveat is, however, to be provided to the effect that this chapter will deal only with the supremacy of law made under the first pillar.

## THE ESTABLISHMENT OF THE DOCTRINE OF SUPREMACY

### The nature of the Community legal order

As detailed above, there is only vague guidance provided within the EC Treaty as to the nature of the relationship between Community and national law. However, the European Court of Justice was quick to elaborate upon a vision of how it perceived the "nature" of Community law. It did so in the influential judgment of *Van Gend en Loos* (Case 26/62):

> "the Community constitutes a new legal order of international law for the benefit of which the States have limited their sovereign rights, albeit within limited fields, and the subjects of which comprise not only Member States but also their nationals".

The judgment is significant as it sets out the Court's view of the legal order created by the Treaty of Rome. This legal order is unlike anything that has previously existed in international law and, as noted by the Court, is based upon the idea that the Member States have limited their sovereign rights in certain areas.

### The establishment of the supremacy of Community law

While the case of *Van Gend en Loos* did not explicitly establish the supremacy of Community law over conflicting national law, its significance to the development of the principle lies in the view taken by the European Court of the "special" nature of the legal order created by the EC Treaty. This "vision" was advanced again by the Court in its seminal judgment in *Costa* v *ENEL* (Case 6/64) in which it was held:

> "By contrast with ordinary international treaties, the EEC Treaty has created its own legal system which ... became an integral part of the legal systems of the Member States and which their courts are bound to apply ... The transfer by the States from their domestic legal system to the Community legal system of the rights and obligations arising under the Treaty carries with it a permanent limitation of their sovereign rights, against which a subsequent unilateral act incompatible with the concept of the Community cannot prevail ...
>
> [T]he law stemming from the Treaty, an independent source of law, could not, because of its special and original nature, be overridden by domestic legal provisions, however framed, without being deprived of its character as Community law and without the legal basis of the Community itself being called into question."

The case of *Costa* therefore marked the first statement of confirmation by the European Court of Justice that Community law does in fact enjoy supremacy over conflicting national law. The reasoning advanced by the Court in *Costa* is interesting, as it very much builds upon the idea advanced in its judgment in *Van Gend en Loos* that the Community constitutes a "new legal order". This new order has become an integral part of the legal systems of the Member States and so the very effectiveness of Community law would be deprived if it were possible for the Member States to issue Acts which are incompatible with Community law.

## WHICH SOURCES OF COMMUNITY LAW HAVE SUPREMACY?

All sources of Community law enjoy supremacy over conflicting national law. This means that not only do the provisions of the Treaties have supremacy, but secondary legislation such as Directives, Regulations and Decisions does as well.

## DOES COMMUNITY LAW HAVE SUPREMACY OVER ALL SOURCES OF NATIONAL LAW?

The ECJ has held that Community law has supremacy over all conflicting forms of national law. This is regardless of whether the national rule in question was adopted subsequent to the entry into force of the Treaty, as was the scenario in the case of *Costa v ENEL*. Furthermore, the doctrine of supremacy applies irrespective of whether the Community law in question is directly effective (see Chapter 4). Indeed, as will be exemplified, EC law even has primacy over national constitutional provisions.

## THE SUPREMACY OF COMMUNITY LAW OVER NATIONAL CONSTITUTIONAL PROVISIONS

The primacy of Community law over national constitutional provisions has proved to be a very controversial subject. The ECJ first approached the issue in the seminal case *Internationale Handelsgesellschaft* (Case 11/70) which concerned a number of Community Regulations, the provisions of which were argued to be in breach of certain fundamental principles associated with the German Constitution. A German administrative court referred a series of questions under the preliminary ruling procedure outlined in Art 234 EC (see Chapter 9) to the European Court of Justice on the validity of the contested Community provisions.

In issuing a preliminary ruling on the German court's request, the European Court held that the validity of Community law measures can *only* be judged in light of Community law. As such, the validity of Community law cannot be determined by reference to its adherence to national constitutional traditions. Accordingly:

> "[T]he validity of a Community measure or its effect within a Member State cannot be affected by allegations that it runs counter to either fundamental rights as formulated by the constitution of that State or the principles of a national constitutional structure."

## WHAT IS THE ROLE OF NATIONAL COURTS IN APPLYING THE DOCTRINE OF SUPREMACY?

In the event of a conflict between Community law and national law, the domestic rule in question must be set aside. In this regard, the European Court of Justice has consistently held that the supremacy of Community law occurs automatically. This means that there is no need for a national court, when faced with a conflicting national law, to wait for the legislature or indeed a higher national court to set the national law concerned aside. An illustration of the approach taken by the ECJ in this regard can be found in *Simmenthal* (Case 106/77) which concerned a series of Italian measures that imposed charges upon meat products imported from other Member States. The rules were quite clearly in breach of Community law and the European Court of Justice had previously given a ruling to this effect. However, the question facing the national court was whether it should simply set the measures aside or wait for the Italian Constitutional Court to give judgment. The national court referred its query to the ECJ, which responded to the effect that when:

> "[A] national court which is called upon, within the limits of its jurisdiction, to apply provisions of Community law is under a duty to give full effect to those provisions, if necessary refusing of its own motion to apply any conflicting provisions of national legislation ... it is not necessary for the court to request or await the prior setting aside of such provision by legislative or other constitutional means."

Thus in *Simmenthal*, the ECJ held that when a national law is found to conflict with Community law, it should be set aside immediately. In *R v Secretary of State for Transport, ex parte Factortame* (Case C-213/89) the

European Court went even further, determining that a provision of national law which may potentially be in conflict with Community law should be temporarily set aside until such time as a full judgment could be given on the issue. At the time of the *Factortame* litigation, national rules existent within the UK prevented the temporary setting aside of the particular law in question. The ECJ held that this was of no consequence, deciding that;

> "[T]he full effectiveness of Community law would be just as much impaired if a rule of national law could prevent a court seised of a dispute governed by Community law from granting interim relief in order to ensure the full effectiveness of the judgment to be given on the existence of the rights claimed under Community law. It follows that a court which in those circumstances would grant interim relief, if it were not for a rule of national law, is obliged to set aside that rule."

In *Commission v France* (Case 167/73) the European Court held that even if a national rule which conflicted with Community law was not actually applied in practice, it should still be repealed. The case concerned a French rule which set down that three-quarters of the crew on French merchant naval boats should be French nationals. This rule was held to be a breach of what is now Art 39 EC on the free movement of workers and so was required to be set aside.

However, the European Court has acknowledged that there may be limits to the application of supremacy. As set out, where there is a conflict between national and Community law, the provisions of the former should be set aside. However, situations may arise in which the national rules are applied in settings independent of Community law. In such a scenario, there will be no conflict between national and Community law with the consequence that the national law may be upheld. However, this will only be in relation to situations which do not come within the scope of European law: *Ministero Delle Finanze v IN.CO.GE.'90 Srl* (Cases C-10–22/97).

## SUPREMACY AND THE UNITED KINGDOM

### The reception of Community law into the United Kingdom

The United Kingdom was not an original member of the European Communities. To facilitate its entry, the UK passed into force the European Communities Act 1972. Section 2(1) of this Act provides explicit recognition to the direct effect of Community law, detailing that the "rights, powers, liabilities, obligations and restrictions from time to time created or arising by or under the Treaties ... shall be recognised and available in law, and be enforced, allowed and followed accordingly". Under s 2(4) of the 1972 Act, it is enacted that the application of Community law is in preference to any domestic Act "passed or to be passed". Through this and other provisions of the 1972 Act, the principle of the supremacy of Community law was incorporated into the domestic law of the UK. This enactment was not, however, without its problems.

A fundamental doctrine of UK constitutional law is the legislative supremacy of Parliament. This is sometimes referred to as "parliamentary sovereignty". The concept of parliamentary sovereignty represents the theory that Parliament has (almost) unlimited legislative authority. In principle, this means that no Parliament is able to enact a rule which would bind future Parliaments, as this would interfere with the latter's legislative authority. However, the recognition of the doctrine of supremacy in the European Communities Act did just that. In essence, the 1972 Act bound future Parliaments to adhere to the doctrine of supremacy and thereby recognise the authority of subsequent Community Acts.

So the question facing the UK judiciary in the early years following the UK's accession was whether the European Communities Act 1972 was merely an "ordinary" statute which could impliedly be repealed by a later Act of Parliament. If this was the case, then adherence to the doctrine of supremacy would be impossible.

The UK judiciary initially sought to interpret domestic law in line with Community law; however, this approach, termed "harmonious construction", did not fully adhere to the doctrine of supremacy. This was because there were limits to the extent to which such interpretation could be successful given that, in the event of conflict between national and Community law, it will not always be possible for harmonious interpretation to give effect to the latter.

The UK judiciary eventually accepted the full supremacy of Community law in a number of cases which have had lasting consequences for the relationship between Community law and UK domestic law. The first of these judgments was issued by the House of Lords in the case of *R* v *Secretary of State for Transport, ex parte Factortame Ltd (No 2)* (1991) which concerned an application for a temporary injunction against the enforcement of provisions under the Merchant Shipping Act 1988. The case is significant for the House of Lords' pronouncement that the supremacy of Community law over national law was well established by the time that the UK joined the Community. As a consequence:

"[W]hatever limitation of its sovereignty Parliament accepted when it enacted the European Communities Act 1972 it was entirely voluntary. Under the terms of the Act of 1972 it has always been clear that it was the duty of a United Kingdom court, when delivering final judgment, to override any rule of national law found to be in conflict with any directly enforceable rule of Community law". (per Lord Bridge)

The judgment in *Factortame (No 2)* was followed in *R v Secretary of State for Employment, ex parte Equal Opportunities Communities Commission ("EOC")* (1995), which centred upon an application for judicial review of an Act of Parliament which the applicants contended was in breach of Community law. The Secretary of State for Employment argued that the UK judiciary did not have the power to make a finding that the UK was in breach of its obligations under Community law. However, the House of Lords declared the case of *Factortame* as a precedent in favour of its authority to conduct such a review. This arguably set the scene for the case of *Thoburn v Sunderland City Council* (2002), which concerned the prosecution of a number of individuals – the so-called "Metric Martyrs" – for selling products using imperial rather than metric measurements, which acts were in contravention of European law. The judge in this case, Laws LJ, held that the European Communities Act 1972 is unlike ordinary statutes which may be impliedly repealed by later Acts of Parliament. Rather:

"All the specific rights and obligations which EU law creates are by the 1972 Act incorporated into our domestic law and rank supreme: that is, anything in our substantive law inconsistent with any of these rights and obligations is abrogated or must be modified to avoid the inconsistency. This is true even where the inconsistent municipal provision is contained in primary legislation. (2) The 1972 Act is a constitutional statute: that is, it cannot be impliedly repealed. (3) The truth of (2) is derived, not from EU law, but purely from the law of England: the common law recognises a category of constitutional statutes."

By according the European Communities Act 1972 the rank of a "constitutional statute", Laws LJ therefore provided the necessary rationale to refute the application of the doctrine of implied repeal which only applies to "ordinary" statutes. In the view of Laws LJ, since the 1972 Act has "constitutional" status, there is therefore no bar to the UK courts accepting the doctrine of supremacy in relation to Community law. However, it is notable that, in *Thoburn*, Laws LJ recognised that there are limits to the acceptance by the UK of the doctrine of supremacy. Such limits would arise in the following hypothetical scenario. Where:

> "[A] European measure was seen to be repugnant to a fundamental or constitutional right guaranteed by the law of England, a question would arise whether the general words of the 1972 Act were sufficient to incorporate the measure and give it overriding effect in domestic law. But that is very far from this case."

It is clear, then, that the UK judiciary has accepted the doctrine of supremacy, although the comments of Laws LJ in the case of *Thoburn* would seem to suggest that there may be limits to such acceptance. A similar pronouncement has been given by the *Bundesverfassungsgericht*, Germany's highest court, in the case of *Brunner* v *European Union Treaty* (1994). While it is extremely unlikely that national courts would ever refuse to recognise the supremacy of Community law, the previous two cases are illustrative of the constant dialogue that exists between national and Community courts.

## CONCLUSION

The above examination of the case law of the ECJ illustrates that Community law has supremacy over all conflicting national law. The now abandoned Constitutional Treaty would have incorporated the principle of supremacy into the main body of the Treaty, with Art I-6 providing that "[t]he Constitution and law adopted by the institutions of the Union in exercising competences conferred on it shall have primacy over the law of Member States". However, under the Treaty of Lisbon, reference to the primacy of European law is dropped from the main text and transferred to a Declaration appended to the Treaty. This Declaration confirms the existing case law on the issue of the relationship between Community and national law and reads as follows:

> "The conference recalls that, in accordance with well settled case law of the EU Court of Justice, the Treaties, and the law adopted by the Union on the basis of the Treaties, have primacy over the law of Member States, under the conditions laid down by said case law."

## Essential Facts

- Community law enjoys supremacy over national law.
- Supremacy requires that in the event of inconsistency between Community and domestic law, the conflicting provisions of the latter are to be set aside.
- The doctrine of supremacy applies over all provisions of national law, including those rules of a constitutional nature as well as fundamental rights provisions.
- As a consequence of the operation of supremacy, the validity of Community law can be judged only by the Community courts. National courts are not permitted to review the validity of Community rules.
- All national courts have recognised and apply the principle of the supremacy of European law. However, such acceptance is not always unconditional.

## Essential Cases

**Costa v ENEL (1964)**: Community law has supremacy over conflicting provisions of national law.

**Internationale Handelsgesellschaft (1970)**: Community law has supremacy over conflicting rules of a constitutional nature.

**Simmenthal (1978)**: the supremacy of Community law occurs automatically

**Kapferer v Schlank & Schick GmbH (2006)**: the application of supremacy does not require final judicial decisions of a national court to be set aside.

**R v Secretary of State for Transport, ex parte Factortame Ltd (No 2) (1991)**: the House of Lords has recognised the application of the doctrine of supremacy and has created new remedies at the domestic level to give such primacy effect.

# 7 DIRECT EFFECT

## INTRODUCTION

The concept of direct effect is central to European law and, while the proper definition to be ascribed to the concept is somewhat disputed, in general it is understood to refer to the notion that if a provision of Community law has direct effect, it gives rise to rights which can be relied upon by individuals in front of their national courts.

Direct effect is an important complement to the supremacy of Community law. Indeed, if individuals were unable to rely upon the provisions of Community law before their national courts, the operation of the doctrine of supremacy would be without substance. It is therefore important to see the "linkages" which exist between the two principles and how each serves to ensure that individuals are able to rely upon and receive benefit from the rights granted to them under Community law.

The EC Treaty does not explicitly provide for the possibility of direct effect. The concept, like that of supremacy, is a judge-made doctrine, enunciated by the ECJ to allow individuals to rely upon the rights granted to them under Community law. Furthermore, not all provisions of Community law are directly effective. The Court has elaborated a number of "tests" which should to be taken into account when considering whether a particular Community law has direct effect. This chapter will examine the case law of the Court in relation to direct effect before considering which provisions of Community law are capable of direct effect.

## THE DEVELOPMENT OF THE PRINCIPLE OF DIRECT EFFECT

The most important case in the development of direct effect is that of *Van Gend en Loos* (Case 26/62). The facts of the case were rather mundane and involved a dispute as to whether an import duty charged by the Dutch authorities was contrary to what was then Art 12 EEC (current Art 25 EC). The issue was referred to the ECJ by way of a request for a preliminary ruling (see Chapter 9) on whether a private individual could rely upon the provisions of Art 12 EEC in challenging the imposition of the import tariff.

The judgment of the ECJ in the case of *Van Gend en Loos* was a landmark decision in which it was detailed that "Community law ... not only imposes obligations on individuals, but it is also intended to confer upon them rights which become part of their legal heritage". The Court reasoned that since individuals were granted rights under Community law, they must also be able to enforce these rights in front of their national courts, thereby paving the way for the creation of direct effect.

### What other reasons did the Court give for creating the doctrine of direct effect?

The Court in *Van Gend en Loos* adopted what is termed a teleological approach to its interpretation of Community law. This meant that the Court, rather than focusing solely upon the text of the Treaty, also looked to its "spirit and aims". This methodology has been the subject of much criticism since the end result of this style of interpretation was the adoption of a vision of a legal order which the Member States did not necessarily endorse.

In addition to its adoption of a teleological method of interpretation, the Court was keen to identify the practical purpose of direct effect. It noted in its judgment that granting individuals the competence to enforce Community law in their national courts also performed an important supervisory function. In essence, the creation of direct effect entrusts individuals with the power to ensure that Member States actually comply with their obligations under Community law. This theme of "effective supervision" of Member State commitments is something that will be explored further in Chapter 8 on state liability.

### What conditions exist in relation to the operation of direct effect?

As set out in the judgment of *Van Gend en Loos* and developed in subsequent case law, in order for a provision of Community law to be capable of direct effect, it must be:

- clear, precise and unambiguous;
- unconditional;
- not dependent upon further action being taken by Community or national authorities.

A further condition alluded to in the judgment of *Van Gend en Loos*, that the provision must be "negative" in order to give rise to direct effect, has subsequently been dropped. It should, however, be noted that some commentators now feel that the "real" test for operation of direct effect is one of justiciability; that is, does the provision confer rights upon individuals which are capable of enforcement?

If a provision of Community law does not meet the criteria outlined above, it may not be directly relied upon by an individual in front of his or her national court. The provision may, however, be capable of indirect effect, a concept which we will examine later in this chapter.

## Which provisions of Community law are capable of direct effect?

As detailed in the introduction to this chapter, not all provisions of Community law are directly effective. In addition to the conditions set out in the case of *Van Gend en Loos*, the Court has also elaborated upon a series of rules regarding the direct effect of particular sources of Community law. We will deal with each of these sources in turn. However, before doing so it is important to consider a distinction that exists in the operation of direct effect: the distinction between vertical and horizontal direct effect:

- **vertical direct effect** may be defined as the capacity to enforce a provision of Community law in an action against a Member State or an entity of that state;
- **horizontal direct effect** refers to the ability of an individual to rely upon a provision of Community law in an action against another private individual.

The distinction between horizontal and vertical forms of direct effect is *not* one of mere semantics. Whether a law is capable of horizontal/vertical direct effect has consequences for individual litigants. For example, if the law in question does not have horizontal direct effect, an individual will not be able to rely upon its provisions as against another private person. This will have ramifications for the legal remedies available and may even prove a decisive element in relation to the final judgment. Therefore, in the following examination, consideration will be given to the distinction between horizontal and vertical direct effects.

## Are provisions of the EC Treaty capable of direct effect?

The case of *Van Gend en Loos* was concerned with the direct effect of (ex) Art 12 EEC (current Art 25 EC). As a consequence, it can be concluded that Articles of the EC Treaty are capable of direct effect provided that they satisfy the other criteria set out in *Van Gend en Loos*.

Treaty Articles are potentially capable of both horizontal and direct effect, and the subsequent case law of the Court has helped to identify which provisions of the Treaty are capable of direct effect and against whom they will be directly effective.

## Is Community secondary legislation capable of direct effect?

Article 249 EC establishes Community competence to enact three forms of binding EC legislation: Regulations, Directives and Decisions.

### The direct effect of Regulations

Article 249 EC provides:

> "A Regulation shall have general application. It shall be binding in its entirety and directly applicable in all Member States."

You will notice that Regulations are "directly applicable". It is important to distinguish between the concepts of direct effect and direct applicability. Direct applicability refers to the notion that the provisions of a Regulation *automatically* become part of the national law of Member States and therefore do not require implementing legislation. Direct effect, while a related concept, mandates that nationals can then rely on those provisions in front of their national courts. According to the ECJ in *Amsterdam Bulb BV* (Case 50/76):

> "[The] Direct application of a Community regulation means that its entry into force and its application in favour of or against those subject to it are independent of any measure of reception into national law."

Since Regulations automatically become part of national law, the Court has had no problem with declaring that they are capable of direct effect so long as the provision in question satisfies the criteria listed above: *Commission* v *Italy* (Case 39/72).

### The direct effect of Decisions

Article 249 EC provides:

> "A decision shall be binding in its entirety upon those to whom it is addressed."

Unlike Regulations, Decisions do not have "general application". What this means is that the provisions of a Decision will be binding only upon the addressee of the measure. In *Grad v Finanzamt Traunstein* (Case 9/70), the Court confirmed that a Decision will potentially be capable of direct effect but only against its addressee. The practical consequence of this is that if a Decision is addressed to a private individual, it may be relied upon in an action against them but not in proceedings against a Member State. However, if the Decision is addressed to a Member State, the provisions of that Decision can be relied upon in an action against that Member State, but not in an action against another individual.

## The direct effect of Directives

Under Art 249 EC, a Directive is noted to be "binding as to the result to be achieved upon each Member State to which it is addressed but shall leave to the national authorities the choice of form and method". Pursuant to this, Member States are required to transpose the requirements of a Directive into their own national law. Since the choice of "form and method" of implementation is left open to the Member State concerned, it enjoys some discretion with regard to how it transposes the Directive into national law. It should, however, be noted that this discretion does not extend to a right of Member States to implement the Directive only partially or indeed not to implement the Directive at all. Thus, in the words of the Advocate General in *Enka* (Case 38/77) at 2226:

> "[Article 249 EC] leaves to each Member State the choice of 'form and methods' whereby it is to give effect to a directive, [but] does not allow it the choice of not giving effect to the directive at all, or of giving effect to it only in part ... On the contrary [a Member State] that fails fully to give effect to a directive is in breach of the Treaty."

The Member States that are the addressees of the Directive will be granted a period of time within which they will be required to transpose its provisions into national law. If a Member State transposes the provisions of a Directive into national law, the national implementing measures can be relied upon in any dispute. The question as to the direct effect of Directives generally arises only when either the Directive has not been adequately implemented into national law or it has not been incorporated at all. If this is the case, then the applicant *may* be able to rely directly upon the provisions of the Directive itself if the provision in question satisfies the criteria for direct effect elucidated upon by the European Court of Justice in cases such as *Van Gend en Loos*. However, the ability to rely upon the provisions of a Directive in a case heard before a national court depends upon the identity of the other party to the dispute. This issue will be considered below.

## DIRECT EFFECT AND DIRECTIVES: THE PROBLEM OF HORIZONTAL AND VERTICAL DIRECT EFFECT

The provisions of a Directive are capable of enforcement by natural or legal persons against the state or its emanations. To this end, it can be said that Directives are capable of vertical direct effect. This is apparent from the case of *Van Duyn* v *Home Office* (Case 41/71) which centred upon the provisions of Directive 64/221. This permitted Member States to refuse entry to other EC nationals but only on public policy, public security and public health grounds. The applicant, Mrs Van Duyn, was a member of the Church of Scientology and had been refused entry to the UK to take up work with the Church. The UK had based its refusal upon public policy grounds but the problem was that the Directive expressly noted that measures taken on such grounds must be founded upon the "personal conduct" of the individual concerned. She wished to invoke the provisions of the Directive to challenge the UK's decision, alleging that it was taken not on the grounds of her own personal conduct but rather as a consequence of the UK Government's general distaste for the Church of Scientology. The question for the European Court was whether she could rely upon the provisions of the Directive in action against the UK. The Court answered in the affirmative:

> "It would be incompatible with the binding effect attributed to a directive by Article (249) to exclude, in principle, the possibility that the obligation which it imposes may be invoked by those concerned. In particular, where the Community authorities have, by directive, imposed on Member States the obligation to pursue a particular course of conduct, the useful effect of such an act would be weakened if individuals were prevented from relying on it before their national courts and if the latter were prevented from taking it into consideration as an element of Community law."

### Has the Court imposed any restrictions upon the direct effect of Directives?

One restriction which the Court has imposed upon the operation of direct effect is that of a temporal variety. You will remember that a Directive gives a Member State discretion with regard to the "form and method" it chooses to implement the provisions into national law. A time limit will be given for such implementation to occur and, until the expiry of this time limit, a Directive will not be capable of direct effect, as confirmed by the European Court in *Pubblico Ministero v Ratti* (Case 148/78). However, it should be noted that, even before the time limit for implementation has expired, Member States are mandated to "refrain from taking any measures liable to seriously compromise the result prescribed": *Inter-Environnement Wallonie v Region Wallonnie* (Case C-129/96).

In addition, and as alluded to above, a further restriction upon the direct effect of Directives relates to against whom their provisions may be relied upon. While the Court has held that the provisions of a Directive may be relied upon in an action against the state or its emanations, they may *not* be relied upon in a legal action against a natural or legal person. *Directives are hence not capable of horizontal direct effect.* The application of this rule is evident in *Marshall v Southampton & South West Hampshire Area Health Authority* (Case C-152/84).

The proceedings in *Marshall* centred on allegations that the applicant, Mrs Marshall, had been the victim of sex discrimination, contrary to the provisions of Council Directive 76/207/EEC on Equal Treatment. Mrs Marshall sought to rely upon the provisions of the Directive in an action against her employer, a local Health Authority. In response to the action, her employers argued that the provisions of the Directive could not be relied upon against them since the provisions of a Directive were justiciable only against the state and not against private individuals. They thus contended that, despite their status as a state authority, in their dealings with Mrs Marshall they were acting as employers and not in the capacity of a state body.

The European Court confirmed that the provisions of a Directive are binding only upon the Member State to which it is addressed and cannot be enforced against a private individual. However, the Court confirmed that a Directive *could* be enforced against the state regardless of the capacity in which it was acting. The end result of this was that Mrs Marshall could in fact rely upon the provisions of the Directive against her employer. In the words of the Court in *Marshall*:

"With regard to the argument that a directive may not be relied on against an individual, it must be emphasised that according to [Article 249] the binding nature of a directive, which constitutes the basis [for its direct effect] exists only in relation to each Member State to which it is addressed. It follows that a directive may not of itself impose obligations on an individual and that a provision of a directive may not be relied on as against such a person."

While the findings of the Court were advantageous to Mrs Marshall, the downside to the judgment was the Court's confirmation that the provisions of a Directive cannot be enforced against private individuals. Thus, had Mrs Marshall's employers been a private company rather than a public body, she would not have been able to rely upon the provisions of the Equal Treatment Directive in an action against them.

### Why did the Court impose a bar upon the horizontal direct effect of Directives?

The responsibility for implementing a Directive lies with the Member State concerned. One of the central reasons for allowing Directives to be enforced against Member States was the idea that they should not be able to rely upon their own failure to implement a Directive. What this means is that a Member State should not be able to escape liability which would otherwise have arisen under the Directive simply because it has not implemented it. However, this "estoppel"-type argument cannot be applied to bolster the case for horizontal direct effect. As a consequence, it is apparent that the European Court is reluctant to impose upon individuals obligations which have been addressed to the Member States.

## GETTING ROUND THE PROHIBITION ON HORIZONTAL DIRECT EFFECT

The problem with the ECJ's finding that Directives are capable of only vertical direct effect is that the capacity to enforce the provisions of a Directive is dependent upon the identity of the person against whom the action is being taken. This is a far from perfect scenario which has the potential to lead to legal uncertainty and arbitrary injustice. As a consequence, the ECJ has elaborated upon a number of "strategies" to alleviate the impact of its finding that Directives lack horizontal direct effect.

### Strategy one: "emanations of the state"

The first device elaborated upon by the Court to lessen the impact of its ruling in *Marshall* that Directives are only directly effective against the state was to interpret the notion of the "state" in the widest possible way. Given that the modern state comprises a myriad of bodies with complex links to central government, such a wide interpretation is required in order to ensure that individuals are able to enforce their Community law rights in front of their national courts. Thus, in *Fratelli Constanzo SpA* v *Comune di Milano* (Case 103/88), the ECJ held that the state, for the purposes of vertical direct effect, includes "all organs of the administration, including decentralised authorities such as municipalities".

In *Foster* v *British Gas* (Case 188/89) the European Court provided guidance upon which types of organisation will be considered "emanations of the state". The case concerned the question of whether a recently privatised but previously state-owned utilities company could fall within the definition of the state or its emanations. The ECJ directed that relevant considerations to be taken into account in such an assessment include whether the body has been granted authority to provide a "public" service under the control of the state and whether it has special powers beyond those normally granted to individuals to assist its performance of its public service functions. While the Court's assessment in *Foster* does not provide a definitive statement of the nature of a state body, the reasoning advanced has proved authoritative. The advantage of the reasoning of the Court in *Foster* is that it encompasses quite a wide definition of the state and its emanations and thereby helps to strengthen the protection granted to individuals to enforce their rights under Community law before their national courts.

## Strategy two: the creation of the concept of indirect effect

The second mechanism created by the Court to ease the impact of the *Marshall* judgment is its formulation of the concept of "indirect effect" which mandates national courts to interpret and apply national law in line with the Community law. By extension, this imposes an obligation upon national courts to interpret national law in line with the provisions of an unimplemented or inadequately implemented Directive. This concept is often referred to as the "interpretative obligation" and was first elaborated upon in *Von Colson & Kamann* v *Land Nordrhein-Westfalen* (Case 14/83). The case, like that of *Marshall*, concerned the Equal Treatment Directive. This had not been implemented properly into national law and so a question was referred to the ECJ as to whether the applicants could rely upon the provisions of the Directive in a sex discrimination action.

The European Court held that national courts are to be considered as entities of the state and so are responsible for ensuring adherence to Community law. Accordingly, the national court was directed to interpret national legislation in line with the aims of the Directive so as to give them full effect.

"[The obligation] ... to achieve the result envisaged by the directive and their duty under [Article 10 EC] to take all appropriate measures ... to ensure the fulfilment of that obligation, is binding on all the authorities of Member States including, for matters within their jurisdiction, the courts. It follows that, in applying the national law and in particular the provisions of national law specifically introduced in order to implement (the Directive), national courts are required to interpret their national law in the light of the wording and the purpose of the directive."

However, the case of *Von Colson* concerned an action taken against an emanation of the state. To this end, following the judgment, it was unclear whether the "interpretative obligation" applied in relation to disputes between two private parties. The ECJ addressed such questions in *Marleasing SA* v *La Comercial Internacional de Alimentación* (Case C-106/89).

The case of *Marleasing* concerned a dispute which centred upon the provisions of an unimplemented Directive. The action was between two private parties and so the Directive was not capable of direct effect. The question asked of the European Court of Justice was whether the interpretative obligation applied in relation to "horizontal" disputes between private parties. That is, does the national court, when presiding over a dispute between individuals, have a responsibility to interpret national law in light of the provisions of an unimplemented or improperly implemented Directive?

The European Court of Justice answered in the affirmative and found that the interpretative obligation was applicable to proceedings involving private individuals. This obligation applies even in relation to national legislation with no explicit link to the Directive and so includes domestic law which entered into force prior to the Directive. However, the Court noted that national courts are only required "so far as was possible" to interpret national law in this manner. The Court therefore indicated that there may be limits to the interpretative obligation, a fact which was later confirmed in its case law.

### Limits to the doctrine of indirect effect

The limits of interpretative obligation upon national courts are apparent from subsequent case law of the ECJ, a brief synopsis of which is set out below:

**Wagner Miret (Case C-334/92)** This case concerned the provisions of Directive 80/987 which mandated Member States to establish a compensation fund for workers in the event of their employer becoming insolvent. Wagner Miret was employed as a senior manager by a Spanish company which subsequently went bankrupt. He was unable to receive compensation from the fund set up by the Spanish Government under the Directive because the Spanish fund did not provide compensation to those employed at the level of senior manager. To this end, Wagner Miret contested his exclusion from the compensation scheme. The ECJ held that the Directive in question was not precise enough to be directly effective. It then went on to find that the doctrine of indirect effect was also not applicable since it was not possible to read the Spanish implementing provisions to include Wagner Miret within its sphere of application.

*Kolpinghuis Nijmegen (Case 80/96)* The ECJ imposed an additional limit on the operation of indirect effect by prohibiting the interpretation of national law in line with Community law where this would lead to the imposition of criminal liability.

*Konstantinos Adeneler et al* v *Ellinikos Organismos Galaktos (Case C-212/04)* The ECJ held that the obligation upon national courts to interpret domestic law in light of the provisions of a Directive exists only upon the expiry of the time limit imposed for its implementation.

### Strategy three: the creation of state liability

The principle of state liability refers to the notion that Member States may be liable in damages for breach of their obligations under Community law. One such breach which may give rise to a claim for damages is the failure by a state adequately to implement the provisions of a Directive within the prescribed time limit. The principle of state liability will be dealt with more fully in the next chapter but at this juncture it is important to note that individuals who incur loss as a result of the failure of a Member State to transpose the provisions of a Directive into national law may be able to recover damages even if the provision in question is not capable of direct/indirect effect.

### A FINAL COMMENT UPON THE "CREATION" OF DIRECT AND INDIRECT EFFECT

In Chapter 3, the role of the European Court was examined and the significance of its role in the process of European integration was reflected upon. The importance of this role is perhaps best exemplified by the ECJ's "creation" of the doctrines of supremacy, direct effect and indirect effect. Each of these doctrines was formulated during a period of considerable legislative inertia as a consequence of the Luxembourg Accords. As a result of the promotion of these doctrines by the Court, individuals were given the right to rely upon Community law provisions in front of their national courts. These developments have proved integral to the development of Community law and indeed the advancement of the European "project".

## Essential Facts

- "Direct effect" refers to the notion that certain provisions of Community law may be relied upon by individuals in front of their national courts.

- Not all provisions of Community law are capable of direct effect. The Court has elaborated numerous conditions which must be fulfilled before a provision may be directly effective.

- A provision of Community law must be clear, precise, unambiguous and not dependent upon any further implementing legislation before it can give rise to direct effect.

- Articles of the EC Treaty may produce both vertical and horizontal direct effect.

- The provisions of a Regulation are capable of both vertical and horizontal direct effect.

- A decision may be enforced against its addressee.

- A Directive is capable of only vertical direct effect. This means that the provisions of a Directive may be relied upon only as against the state or its emanations. In addition, a Directive becomes capable of direct effect only once the time limit for its implementation has expired.

- The provisions of a Directive may not be applied in a horizontal relationship.

- The European Court of Justice has developed three strategies to overcome the prohibition it has placed upon the horizontal direct effect of directives:

- it has provided a very broad definition of the state for the purposes of the operation of vertical direct effect;
- it has elaborated upon the doctrine of indirect effect which requires national courts to interpret national law in conformity with Community law;
- it allows damages to be sought against the state in the event that it has failed to implement or has incorrectly implemented the provisions of a directive.

## Essential Cases

**Van Gend en Loos (1963)**: established that provisions of the EC Treaty are capable of direct effect.

**Leonesio v Italian Ministry of Agriculture (1972)**: Regulations are capable of direct effect.

**Grad v Finanzamt Traunstein (1970)**: Decisions are capable of direct effect against their addressee.

**Pubblico Ministero v Ratti (1979)**: the provisions of a Directive are capable of direct effect only once the time limit for implementation has expired.

**Van Duyn v Home Office (1974)**: the provisions of a Directive may be vertically directly effective.

**Marshall v Southampton & South West Hampshire Area Health Authority (1986)**: Directives do not produce horizontal direct effect.

**Foster v British Gas (1990)**: the ECJ has elucidated upon its own broad definition of the state and its emanations for the purposes of vertical direct effect.

**Von Colson & Kamann v Land Nordrhein-Westfalen (1984)**: national courts are under an "interpretative obligation". As such, they are required to read and apply national law in line with Community law.

**Marleasing SA v La Comercial Internacional de Alimentación (1990)**: the interpretative obligation imposed upon national courts applies even in relation to disputes between two private individuals.

**Kolpinghuis Nijmegen (1987)**: national courts are not required to interpret national law in line with Community law where the effect would be to impose criminal liability upon an individual.

# 8 STATE LIABILITY

## WHAT IS STATE LIABILITY?

State liability is a doctrine created by the European Court of Justice to ensure the compliance of Member States with their obligations under Community law. It refers to the principle that Member States may be liable for loss and damage caused to individuals as a result of a breach of Community law for which the state can be held responsible.

## Why was it necessary for the ECJ to create the doctrine of state liability?

The creation of the doctrine of state liability is intrinsically linked to efforts on the part of the ECJ to ensure the adherence of Member States to Community law. As we saw in the previous chapter, one of the central rationales behind the creation of the doctrines of direct and indirect effect was that the ECJ wanted to ensure the "effective supervision" of Member States' legal obligations. State liability is yet another mechanism created by the ECJ to ensure that the substance of Community law is not negated by the failure of Member States to comply with their Community law obligations.

## Did the Court not do enough to ensure that Member States adhere to their obligations under Community law by creating the doctrines of direct and indirect effect?

Direct effect and indirect effect operate as complements to the doctrine of supremacy and are two methods which the European Court of Justice has developed to allow individuals to enforce their Community law rights before their national courts. Direct and indirect effect therefore provide individuals with a significant avenue of redress whereby they can go in front of their own national court system to enforce the rights granted to them by European law. There are, however, *limits to the operation of direct and indirect effect*.

These limits are apparent from two scenarios:

(1) Consider what would happen if a *Member State* decides *not to implement a Directive and there is no national law in the area of the*

*Directive.* Imagine that the Directive is not clear or precise enough to be capable of direct effect. In addition, since there is no national law in the area covered by the Directive, it would not be possible for the national courts to interpret national law in line with the Directive. The Directive would hence not be capable of indirect effect. *In such a scenario, an individual who is affected by the failure of the Member State to implement the Directive would not have any source of legal recourse under direct or indirect effect.*

(2) In addition, consider the scenario where *a Member State fails to implement a Directive. Again, imagine that there is no applicable national law in the area of the Directive.* However, this time the Directive is clear and precise enough to be capable of direct effect. However, as we know, a Directive can be relied upon only as against the state and its emanations and not against another individual. An affected individual under such a scenario again would *not have any recourse under the law of direct or indirect effect if they are dealing with another private individual.*

As demonstrated by the above scenarios, direct and indirect effect do not provide a "perfect" enforcement mechanism to guarantee Member State observance of Community law. State liability can therefore be considered as an *additional* mechanism created by the Court to ensure the adherence of Member States to their obligations under Community law.

## STATE LIABILITY

The principle of state liability was first elaborated upon in *Francovich and Bonifaci* v *Italian Republic* (Cases C-6/90 and C-9/90). Francovich and the other claimants were a number of Italian nationals who were employed by a company which subsequently went bankrupt. They took an action against Italy for payment of their outstanding wages. The ability to recover such outstanding sums had been provided for by Council Directive 80/987 but the provisions of this had not been implemented by Italy despite the time limit for implementation having expired. The applicants claimed that in the event that they could not rely upon the provisions of the unimplemented Directive to recover the sums owed to them, they should be entitled to damages from the Italian state. Italy had already been criticised for its failure to implement the Directive and had been the subject of separate proceedings by the Commission under Art 226 EC. However, this action was of little practical use to Francovich and the other claimants.

The issue as to whether Francovich and the other claimants could recover the sums owed to them or, alternatively, be awarded damages by Italy was referred to the European Court of Justice, which held that the (unimplemented) Directive in question was not capable of direct effect. The Court also held that indirect effect was not possible since there was no national law in the area and hence nothing to interpret in conformity with the Directive.

The Court found that Italy was responsible for the loss suffered by Francovich and the other claimants. It then went on to hold that the effectiveness of Community law would be negated if the claimants were unable to obtain compensation for their loss. The end result of the Court's judgment was its elaboration of the principle that a Member State can be forced to pay damages to individuals who are affected by its failure to comply with its obligations under Community law. The Court held that to deny the grant of damages would weaken the protection granted to individuals under Community law. The principle of state liability was therefore held to be inherent in the scheme of the Treaty.

### What conditions must exist before the operation of state liability can take effect?

According to the ECJ in *Francovich*:

> "The first of those conditions is that the result prescribed by the directive should entail the grant of rights to individuals. The second condition is that it should be possible to identify the content of those rights on the basis of the provisions of the directive. Finally, the third condition is the existence of a causal link between the breach of the State's obligation and the loss and damage suffered by the injured parties."

These conditions can be summarised as follows:

- the Directive concerned must be intended to grant rights to individuals;
- the content of such rights must be able to be determined from the Directive itself;
- there must be a causal link between the Member State's breach and the loss/damages suffered.

### What is the practical effect of the principle of state liability?

The decision in the case of *Francovich* assists individuals by providing them with the possibility of damages should a Member State be in breach of its general obligations to comply with Community law. The right to damages is intrinsically connected to the supremacy of Community law. Thus, according to Advocate General Léger in *R v Ministry for Agriculture, Fisheries and Food, ex parte Hedley Lomas* (Case C-5/94):

> "Just as individuals are protected by the fact that the court of the administration may disapply legislation, so they must also be protected by reparation of the damage which they have incurred through the application of legislation which ought to have remained a dead letter."

However, not all breaches of Community law will give rise to a case for damages and, as such, various issues were left unaddressed by the *Francovich* judgment. These issues included considerations such as:

- What constitutes the "state" for the purposes of "state liability"?
- What sort of breaches of Community law could arise in a claim for damages?

These questions were answered in a series of later cases, the most significant of which were joined cases *Brasserie du Pêcheur SA v Germany* and *R v Secretary of State for Transport, ex parte Factortame (No 3)* (Cases C-46 and 48/93).

The facts of *Brasserie* relate to a ban imposed by the German authorities upon the selling of Bierre d'Alsace in Germany. The ban had already been the subject of separate legal proceedings under which the ECJ had found Germany to be in breach of Art 28 EC, which provides for the free movement of goods. The second case, *Factortame*, involved a continuation of previous litigation concerning the UK's Merchant Shipping Act 1988. Again, the ECJ had previously held that certain provisions of the Merchant Shipping Act were contrary to European law. Both cases were therefore concerned with breaches of Community law committed by a Member State.

The question for the ECJ in the above joined cases was whether the relevant breaches of Community law could give rise to a claim for damages. After *Francovich*, it was assumed by some commentators that state liability would arise only in relation to the failure of a state to implement a Directive. However, the judgment of the Court in *Brasserie/Factortame* (hereinafter "*Factortame*") held that the principle was much wider than this and potentially could arise in the event of any "sufficiently serious" breach of Community law committed by a Member State.

## Did the *Factortame* litigation add any conditions to the operation of state liability?

The Court in *Factortame* enunciated a number of additional requirements for the operation of state liability:

> "... [C]ommunity law confers a right to reparation where three conditions are met: the rule of law infringed must be intended to confer rights on individuals; the breach must be sufficiently serious; and there must be a direct causal link between the breach of the obligation resting on the State and the damage sustained by the injured parties."

Thus, the breach of Community law must be *sufficiently serious* before liability for damages can be said to arise. As it stands at present, there are now three conditions for the operation of state liability:

- the rule of law infringed must have been intended to confer rights on individuals;
- the breach must be "sufficiently serious";
- there must be a direct causal link between the breach of the obligation resting on the state and the damage sustained by the injured parties.

### What does the term "sufficiently serious" mean?

A breach will be sufficiently serious where the Member State concerned has "*manifestly and gravely*" disregarded the limits of its discretion. As outlined by the European Court of Justice in the case of *Factortame*, the factors which it will take into account in assessing whether such a breach has occurred include:

- *The clarity and precision of the rule breached.* The approach of the Court in relation to this criterion has been that the clearer and more precise the Community law in question, the greater the likelihood that a breach committed by the Member State concerned will be sufficiently serious.

- *The measure of discretion left by that rule to the national or Community authorities.* Where a Member State has been granted a large degree of discretion in relation to its interpretation or implementation of the Community law in question, the Court will in general be reluctant to find that the Member State concerned has manifestly and gravely disregarded the limits of this discretion.

- *Whether the infringement or damage caused was intentional or involuntary.* A breach which is involuntary is less likely to be considered sufficiently serious.

- *Whether the error of law was excusable or inexcusable.* An inexcusable breach will probably be considered "sufficiently serious".

- *If the position taken by a Community institution contributed to the breach.* A breach precipitated by a Community institution will not generally give rise to a claim for damages.

The Court in *Factortame* also held that a breach of Community law will always be "sufficiently serious" where it has continued despite a ruling that an infringement has occurred. Subsequent case law has further elaborated upon the requirements for state liability, particularly the condition that the breach must be "sufficiently serious":

*R v HM Treasury, ex parte British Telecommunications Ltd* (Case C-392/93). This case concerned the incorrect implementation by the UK of a Directive on public procurement. On the particular facts at issue, the ECJ held that a sufficiently serious breach of Community law had not occurred. This was because the UK's interpretation and subsequent implementation of the Directive had been made in good faith. The provisions of the Directive itself were not particularly clear or precise. To this end, the UK was not liable in damages for misunderstanding the requirements involved in implementing the Directive.

*Dillenkofer v Federal Republic of Germany* (Case C-178/94). This case concerned Germany's failure to implement the provisions of a Directive on package holidays within the prescribed time limit. The case is significant as the Court held that the failure to transpose the provisions of a Directive into national law by the designated date will always constitute a "sufficiently serious" breach.

## To which branches of the "state" does the principle of "state liability" apply?

The "state", for the purposes of a claim for damages, is not confined to central government. Rather, whichever organ of the state is responsible for a breach of Community law will potentially be liable under the principle of state liability. This can include national courts, as confirmed by the ECJ in *Köbler v Austria* (Case C-224/01).

The case of *Köbler* centred upon the failure of the highest Austrian administrative court (*Verwaltungsgericht*) to issue a request to the ECJ for a preliminary ruling in relation to a question of Community law. Under Art

234(3) EC, a national court against whose decisions there is no judicial remedy is required to seek a preliminary ruling from the ECJ on a matter of Community law should a decision on the issue be necessary to enable it to give judgment. The operation of the preliminary ruling system will be dealt with in more detail in Chapter 9. However, at this juncture the importance of the case of *Köbler* stems from the ECJ's determination that the actions of a national court can give rise to a claim for damages under the principle of state liability.

The judgment of the ECJ in *Köbler* was followed up in *Traghetti del Mediterraneo SpA* v *Italy* (Case C-173/03). The case centred upon Italian legislation that sought to exclude the decisions of national courts from those acts or omissions which could potentially give rise to an action for damages under the principle of state liability. The ECJ noted that the legislation went against its findings in the case of *Köbler* and as such determined that it was contrary to Community law.

## What other options are available to "police" the enforcement of Community law?

One of the central functions of the Commission is its role as "guardian of the treaties". A central component of this role is the Commission's power under Art 226 EC to bring an action against a Member State for *failure to act*:

### Article 226 EC

"If the commission considers that a Member State has failed to fulfil an obligation under this Treaty it shall deliver a reasoned opinion on the matter after giving the State concerned the opportunity to submit its observations.

If the State concerned does not comply with the opinion within the period laid down by the Commission, the latter may bring the matter before the Court."

Thus, pursuant to Art 226 EC, if the Commission decides that the Member State in question has in some way committed a violation of Community law, it is required to issue a "reasoned opinion" in which it sets out its decision to the Member State concerned. The opinion of the Commission will contain guidelines as to what the Member State is required to do in order to remedy the violation of Community law which has occurred. A time limit for the breach to be remedied will also be specified. If the Member State does not adhere to the recommendations of the opinion within the time frame provided, the Commission may commence enforcement proceedings before the European Court of Justice. The Court will then review the case and issue its judgment. If the Court decides against the Member State and it subsequently fails to comply with the terms of the judgment, the Commission may ask the Court to impose a fine or other penalty upon the Member State concerned.

It is therefore possible for the Commission to take an enforcement action against Member States for failure to "fulfil an obligation". A common reason for such enforcement action against a Member State is for failure to implement a Directive. However, there are a number of problems in relying on such enforcement action to ensure Member States' compliance with their obligations.

### What problems exist in relation to the operation of Art 226 EC?

The use by the Commission of the procedure outlined in Art 226 EC is very politically contentious and is in general used only as a last resort. In relation, the ECJ has repeatedly held that it cannot review the political motivation behind the Commission's decision as to whether or not to utilise the procedure outlined under Art 226 EC. In addition, on a purely procedural level, the Commission cannot take action against every single infraction of Community law. Furthermore, Art 226 EC proceedings may take several years to complete and, while an interim application is possible, these are not always granted.

Due to the problems inherent in the use of Art 226 EC as an enforcement mechanism to promote the adherence of Member States to their Community law obligations, the ECJ has elaborated another method through which to protect the rights of individuals and thereby ensure the effectiveness and uniformity of Community law. As examined above, this mechanism is "state liability".

## CONCLUSION

It is thus apparent that various methods exist to ensure that individuals are able to rely upon the rights granted to them under Community law. These mechanisms may be summarised as follows:

- supremacy;
- direct effect;
- indirect effect;
- state liability.

Each of these judicially created doctrines has served to enhance the effectiveness of Community law and it is clear that each forms an important constitutional principle which lies at the heart of the operation of European law.

---

### Essential Facts

- State liability refers to the principle that Member States may be liable for loss and damage caused to individuals as a result of a breach of Community law for which the state can be held responsible.
- In order for an action for damages under the principle of state liability to arise, three conditions must be fulfilled. They are:
  - the rule of law infringed must have been intended to confer rights on individuals;
  - the breach must be "sufficiently serious". This will occur only when the Member State concerned has manifestly and gravely disregarded the limits of its discretion; and
  - there must be a direct causal link between the breach of Community law committed by the state concerned and the damage caused to the applicants.

---

### Essential Cases

**Francovich and Bonifaci v Italian Republic (1991)**: established the principle of state liability.

**Brasserie du Pêcheur SA v Germany and R v Secretary of State for Transport, ex parte Factortame (No 3) (1996)**: introduced the requirement that the breach of Community law must be "sufficiently serious" before a case for damages under the principle of state liability may be made.

**Dillenkofer v Federal Republic of Germany (1996)**: failure to implement the provisions of a Directive will always constitute a "sufficiently serious" breach.

**Köbler v Austria (2003)**: the actions or omissions of national courts may give rise to an action for damages under the principle of state liability.

# 9 PRELIMINARY RULINGS

## WHAT IS A PRELIMINARY RULING?

Sometimes, national courts will be asked to adjudicate upon a case which involves some aspect of Community law. The national court may be unsure as to the correct interpretation to give to the Community law concerned, or, alternatively, it may be asked to give a decision upon the validity of a Community law act, something which it is not within the competence of a national court to decide.

Article 234 EC allows national courts to seek advice from either the ECJ or the CFI on the validity or interpretation to be given to the Community law act at issue. The request from the national court will be framed as a question or indeed a series of questions. If the ECJ or the CFI decides that a decision on the matter is required in order to enable the national court to give judgment, it will issue what is referred to as a preliminary ruling on the matter.

The preliminary ruling procedure has been referred to on numerous occasions in previous chapters. To this end, its importance to the development of Community law cannot be overestimated. Many of the most significant cases in the evolution of the Community legal system have started off life as a request by a national court for a preliminary ruling on a particular issue of Community law. This chapter will look at the jurisdiction of the Community courts to receive preliminary ruling requests, before going on to examine the operation of the procedure.

## THE PRELIMINARY RULING SYSTEM: THE BASICS

The primary competence of the ECJ to issue preliminary rulings is set out in Art 234 EC, which provides;

> "The Court of Justice shall have jurisdiction to give preliminary rulings concerning:
>   (a) the interpretation of this Treaty;
>   (b) the validity and interpretation of acts of the institutions of the Community and of the ECB;
>   (c) the interpretation of the statutes of bodies established by an act of the Council, where those statutes so provide.
> Where such a question is raised before any court or tribunal of a Member State, that court or tribunal may, if it considers that a decision on the question

is necessary to enable it to give judgment, request the Court of Justice to give a ruling thereon.

Where any such question is raised in a case pending before a court or tribunal of a Member State against whose decisions there is no judicial remedy under national law, that court or tribunal shall bring the matter before the Court of Justice."

## HOW DOES THE PRELIMINARY REFERENCE PROCEDURE WORK IN PRACTICE?

If a question of Community law arises in the course of a dispute before a national court, Art 234 EC allows the domestic court to stay proceedings and seek advice from either the CFI or ECJ on the interpretation or indeed validity of a particular provision of Community law. The CFI or ECJ will then provide a ruling on the question referred. The original national court will then consider the opinion issued by the ECJ/CFI before giving judgment on the dispute. It should therefore be underlined that under the preliminary reference procedure, the Community courts do not function as appellate courts.

The process by which a preliminary ruling is issued can therefore be summarised thus:

(1) There is a case before a national court which involves some aspect of Community law. This may involve a question as to the interpretation or validity of a particular component of Community law.

(2) The national court concerned may then refer the question relating to the interpretation or validity of Community law to the CFI/ECJ.

(3) The CFI/ECJ will then provide an opinion on the question referred by the national court.

(4) The national court will then take into account the CFI/ECJ's opinion in adjudicating upon the dispute at hand.

## THE TREATY OF NICE AND CHANGES TO THE PRELIMINARY REFERENCE PROCEDURE

Until recently, the ECJ had exclusive competence to issue preliminary rulings. However, Art 225(3) EC, introduced by the Treaty of Nice, grants the CFI competence to hear preliminary reference requests as well.

## PURPOSE OF PRELIMINARY REFERENCE

### Ensures dialogue between national and Community courts

The Court of Justice has repeatedly asserted that the preliminary ruling procedure represents a continual process of dialogue between it and national courts. Thus, in the case of *Schmeink & Cofreth and Strobel* (Case C-454/98), the Court of Justice described the preliminary ruling procedure as an "instrument of co-operation" which assists it and the national court "to make direct and complementary contributions to the working out of a decision".

### Uniformity

One central purpose of the preliminary ruling procedure is to ensure that Community law is applied *uniformly*. The procedure helps to ensure uniformity by allowing national courts to seek advice and guidance on particular elements of Community law. Hence, in *Rheinmuhlen-Dusseldorf v Einfuhr- und Vorratstelle für Getreide und Futtermittel* (Case 166/73), the Court of Justice stated that the preliminary ruling procedure is "essential for the preservation of the Community character of the law established by the Treaty and has the object of ensuring that in all circumstances the law is the same in all states of the Community". Similarly, in *ICC v Administrazione delle Finanze* (Case 66/80), the Court of Justice stated that:

> "The main purpose of the powers accorded to the Court by Article (234 EC) is to ensure that Community law is applied uniformly by national courts. Uniform application of Community law is imperative not only when a national court is faced with a rule of Community law the meaning and scope of which needed to be defined; it is just as imperative when the Court is confronted by a dispute as to the validity of an act of the institutions."

### Protection of the individual

The preliminary reference procedure is a vital tool to ensuring that individuals are able to rely upon the rights they have been granted by Community law. It allows individuals to have "indirect' access to the Community courts. Such access is indirect since an action must be taken before a national court before a preliminary reference may be sought. The preliminary ruling procedure therefore acts as a complement to the operation of supremacy and direct effect.

## WHO CAN SEEK A PRELIMINARY RULING?

Article 234 EC details that only courts and tribunals may request a preliminary ruling. Thus, an individual cannot seek clarification on a point of Community law directly from the Community courts. Instead, they would have to take a case before their respective national court system and request that the national court seek a preliminary ruling from the ECJ/CFI.

Thus, while an individual may not seek a preliminary ruling, it is obvious from the text of Art 234 EC that a court within the national judicial structure may make such a request. However, problems have arisen with regard to discerning which bodies may seek a ruling, as certain institutions may not necessarily be called a court or tribunal but may still perform important judicial or quasi-judicial functions. In response, the ECJ has delineated an autonomous Community meaning for a "court" or a "tribunal" under Art 234 EC.

## WHAT IS A "COURT" OR "TRIBUNAL" WITHIN THE MEANING OF ARTICLE 234 EC?

The approach of the ECJ in elucidating upon whether a body is a court or tribunal has been to look at the relevant body's function, composition and jurisdiction. This approach is exemplified by *Vaassen* (Case 61/65), in which the European Court accepted a preliminary reference request from a Dutch social security arbitral tribunal. The factors which the ECJ took into account in determining that the tribunal did come within the scope of Art 234 EC included the fact that it was an independent and permanent body charged with the settlement of disputes and applying rules of national law.

While there exists no concrete definition of which bodies are considered to be courts or tribunals with jurisdiction to seek a preliminary ruling, subsequent case law such as *Dorsch Consult* (Case C-54/96) has seen the ECJ take into account criteria such as the following:

- whether the body in question is independent;
- whether it enjoys compulsory jurisdiction;
- whether proceedings are *inter partes;*
- whether the body applies rules of law;
- whether it is permanent.

## WHAT CAN BE REFERRED TO THE COMMUNITY COURTS UNDER THE PRELIMINARY REFERENCE PROCEDURE?

From a jurisdictional perspective, competence is granted under the EC Treaty to receive requests for a preliminary ruling relating to:

- the interpretation of the EC Treaty;
- the validity and interpretation of acts of the institutions of the Community and of the European Central Bank;
- the interpretation of the statutes of bodies established by an act of the Council, where those statutes so provide.

From a practical viewpoint, the European Court was initially prepared to hear almost all preliminary ruling requests so long as they fell within its jurisdiction. However, as the workload of the ECJ increased, it began to place controls over the "type" of question which could be referred to it.

## CONTROLS UPON THE PRELIMINARY RULING PROCEDURE

The first of these controls relates to the condition that there must be a genuine dispute before the national court/tribunal before a question may be referred to the Community courts. This requirement was elucidated upon in *Foglio* v *Novello (I)* (Case 104/79) in which the parties to the proceedings were arguing over who should pay a levy which they both agreed was imposed in contravention of Community law. The matter was referred by the national court to the ECJ, which declined to exercise jurisdiction since it held that there was no real dispute at issue. This was because both parties agreed that the tax was in breach of Community law. The parties therefore did not require the ECJ to assist them in their interpretation of Community law.

An additional "control" upon the preliminary ruling procedure is that the European Court will also examine whether the question referred by the national court contains the necessary factual and legal background to the case to enable it to give a preliminary ruling. This requirement is exemplified by *Telemarsicabruzzo* v *Circostel* (Cases C-320, 321 and 322/90). In the event that the national court fails to include this information, the European Court of Justice will normally refuse the application

## THE QUESTION OF WHETHER TO SEEK A PRELIMINARY REFERENCE

Should a decision on an issue of Community law prove necessary to enable a national court or tribunal to give judgment, Art 234 EC distinguishes between courts which have *discretion* as to whether or not to seek a preliminary ruling and those which are under an *obligation* to refer a question to the ECJ/CFI.

## THE OBLIGATION TO SEEK A PRELIMINARY RULING UNDER ART 234 EC

### Which courts or tribunals are under an obligation to seek a preliminary reference?

Guidance on this issue is provided in Art 234(3) which details that the obligation applies only to courts/tribunals against whose decision there is no right of appeal. From the outset, questions were raised as to whether this statement applied only to the decisions of final appellate courts or whether it also covers courts deciding a case in the last instance. The distinction is clear if one uses the example of a claim for a very small sum of damages. Such a case will obviously not end up in the House of Lords. So essentially the question was whether Art 234(3) refers to actual courts of last instance in the particular case at issue, or formal courts of final appeal such as the High Court of Justiciary or the House of Lords.

The answer to the above question was provided in *Costa* v *ENEL* (Case C 6/64). In *Costa*, the Italian equivalent of a small claims court was considered a court of last instance because the small sum of money involved in the dispute (equivalent to £1) meant that there was no appeal from the decision of the magistrate. In this case, the ECJ held that the Italian court came within the meaning of a court of last instance since beyond that point in proceedings there was no real avenue of appeal.

### Conditions relating to the obligation to refer

While the text of Art 234(3) EC would seem to impose an obligation upon courts of last instance to ask for a preliminary reference every time a question of Community law arises, this is not actually the case. There are various exceptions to the obligation to refer, which the ECJ has come to recognise.

### Exception one: the "materially identical" case

If the ECJ has already interpreted an identical issue in an earlier case, "the authority of an interpretation under Art 234 EC already given by the Court may deprive the obligation (to refer) from its purpose and thus empty it of substance": *Da Costa* v *Nederlandse Belastingadministratie* (Cases 28, 29 and 30/62).

So, if the point of law is "materially identical" to one already addressed in an earlier preliminary ruling, there is no obligation to refer. There are numerous reasons for the Court's elaboration of this exception to Art 234(3). The primary one relates to the operation of the doctrine of supremacy. Since Community law is to be applied uniformly across all Member States, the existence of a previous reference relating to materially identical issues means that a new reference will not be required. *The obligation to refer, however, is retained when the question at issue concerns the validity of an Act of Community law.* This is because national courts cannot declare Community Acts invalid: *Foto-Frost v Hauptzollamt Lunbeck-Ost* (Case 318/05).

### Exception two: the answer to the question is so obvious as to negate the need for a preliminary reference

The operation of this exception is exemplified by *CILFIT v Ministry of Health* (Case 283/81). This dispute concerned an Italian law which imposed an inspection levy on the import of wool. The law was challenged on the ground that it was incompatible with European law. The Italian Court of last instance considered that the case law on the issue was clear and that the Italian rule was in contravention of Community law. However, it was unsure whether, as a court of final instance, it was still under an obligation to seek a preliminary ruling from the ECJ. The ECJ stated that there is no obligation to refer if the answer was clear, the meaning of the provision at issue obvious or the matter irrelevant to the dispute at hand.

### Summary

It is hence not necessary for a court of last instance to request a preliminary reference in the following scenarios:

- if the question of Community law is not relevant to the actual dispute;
- if the question has already been interpreted by the ECJ;
- if the correct application of Community law is so clear as to leave no room for reasonable doubt. This is an explicit endorsement of the French legal doctrine of *"acte clair"* whereby if the interpretation of a particular provision is clear, there is no need to seek clarification regarding its implementation.

In deciding whether or not to make a request for a preliminary ruling, the ECJ outlined in the above case of *CILFIT* that the national court of last instance must take into account the following conditions:

- whether the "answer" to the matter at issue would be equally obvious to the courts of other Member States as well as the ECJ itself;
- the national court must also be cognisant that legal concepts, particularly those used in Community law, have different meanings across Member States;
- finally, the national court is required to read the provision in its relevant context and to interpret it in line with Community law.

Where the meaning of the Community law in question is not clear, a national court of final instance is not permitted to substitute its own judgment for that of the Community courts. This is illustrated by *Köbler* v *Austria* (Case C-224/01). In this case (see also discussion in Chapter 8 on state liability) an Austrian court of final instance failed to seek a preliminary reference on the proper interpretation to be given to a provision of Community law, on the ground that the operation of the law in question was clear. The applicant, Mr Köbler, claimed that the provision was not clear and was in fact contrary to Community law. The case was decided against him and so he sought damages for the loss he had suffered as a result of the Austrian court's decision that the national law in question was not contrary to Community law. He asserted that the national court concerned should have referred the issue to the ECJ. In this second action by Mr Köbler, the ECJ held that a court of final instance *may* be liable to pay damages under the doctrine of state liability if it fails to request a preliminary reference in circumstances in which the interpretation of Community law was in doubt. It found that the Austrian court had been wrong to find that the meaning of the Community law in question was clear and found that the court concerned should have sought a preliminary reference. However, it did not consider the error committed to be "sufficiently serious" as to give rise to a claim for damages under the principle of state liability. However, in principle it is possible to recover damages for loss occasioned by the failure of a national court to seek a preliminary reference.

## CHANGES TO THE PRELIMINARY REFERENCE PROCEDURE CONTAINED IN THE LISBON TREATY

One significant change to the preliminary ruling process which will occur in the event of the adoption of the Treaty of Lisbon is the introduction of an emergency procedure. This is outlined in Art 267 TFEU which tasks that:

> "If such a question is raised in a case pending before a court or tribunal of a Member State with regard to a person in custody, the Court of Justice of the European Union shall act with the minimum of delay."

In addition, the jurisdiction of the Court under the preliminary reference procedure will be extended so that it will have competence to review the validity or interpretation of acts of not only the institutions, but also the bodies, offices and agencies of the Union.

## THE SIGNIFICANCE OF THE PRELIMINARY REFERENCE PROCEDURE

The preliminary reference procedure has been utilised by the ECJ to build up a significant body of jurisprudence, the effects of which are still markedly evident in the operation of Community law. The Court has been assisted in this by the willingness of national courts to seek preliminary rulings and apply the rulings of the ECJ in domestic cases.

The preliminary reference procedure is also important in the context of granting individuals a right of access, even if an indirect one, to the Community courts. This is particularly relevant should an individual wish to challenge the validity of a Community act. As will be discussed in the next chapter, it is very difficult for a natural or legal person directly to challenge the legality of a Community act under the procedure established for the judicial review of Community decisions under Art 230 EC. The preliminary reference procedure is thus a central mechanism to ensure the protection of individuals who are affected by a particular legal act of the Community but who cannot, for whatever reason, launch an action for judicial review. However, the one drawback to this is that outside of the scenario of a court or tribunal of final instance, there is no obligation for the national court or tribunal to refer a request for a preliminary ruling to the CFI/ECJ. This discretion to refer could potentially deny individual applicants the right of effective legal protection in instances in which they wish to challenge the validity of a Community act. This theme of effective legal protection will be explored in more detail in the next chapter.

## Essential Facts

- The preliminary ruling procedure outlined under Art 234 EC allows national courts to seek advice from either the ECJ or the CFI on the validity or interpretation to be given to the Community law act.
- Only national courts or tribunals may seek a preliminary ruling and the ECJ has provided guidelines upon the types of judicial body which have competence to utilise the procedure under Art 234 EC.
- Article 234 EC makes a distinction between national courts and tribunals which have discretion to refer a question to the Community courts and those which are under an obligation to seek a preliminary ruling.
- Courts of final instance are under an obligation to seek a preliminary ruling under Art 234 EC but there are exceptions to this:
    - where a question of Community law is not relevant to the actual dispute, there will be no obligation to refer;
    - if the question has already been the subject of a ruling by the Community courts, again there will be no obligation to refer;
    - there is no requirement to seek a preliminary ruling if the correct application of Community law is so clear as to leave no room for reasonable doubt.

## Essential Cases

**Vaassen (1966)**: the definition of a court or tribunal within the meaning of Art 234 EC is a Community concept independent of national law.

**Foto–Frost v Hauptzollamt Lunbeck–Ost (1987)**: national courts do not have the authority to declare a Community act invalid.

**Foglio v Novello (I) (1980)**: a preliminary ruling request must emanate from a genuine dispute.

**Da Costa v Nederlandse Belastingadministratie (1963)**: there is no obligation to seek a preliminary ruling on the interpretation of a Community act if a ruling has already been provided on the issue.

**CILFIT v Ministry of Health (1982)**: confirmed that there is no obligation for a national court or tribunal to seek a ruling on the interpretation to be afforded to a Community act where the answer is clear.

# 10  JUDICIAL REVIEW

Article 220 EC directs that "(t)he Court of Justice and the Court of First Instance, each within its jurisdiction, shall ensure that in the interpretation and application of this Treaty the law is observed". Pursuant to this, Art 230 EC provides the European Court of Justice with competence to review the legality of acts adopted by the main Community institutions. Article 225 EC also grants the Court of First Instance the competence to hear applications for judicial review under the procedure outlined in Art 230 EC. The procedure by which this power is exercised is usually referred to as *judicial review*. This chapter will examine the competence of the Community courts to hear actions for judicial review before setting out the rules by which such a case may be taken.

It is to be noted that this chapter will only consider the process by which the Community courts review acts adopted under Pillar I. This is because acts adopted under Pillar II may only exceptionally be subject to an action for judicial review (*Yassin Abdullah Kadi and Al Barakaat International Foundation* v *Council and Commission* (Cases C-402/05 P and C-415/05 P)) while, under Pillar III, only the Commission and the Member States may bring such an action.

## WHY IS THE POSSIBILITY OF JUDICIAL REVIEW SO IMPORTANT?

In Chapters 4 and 5, we examined the capacity of the Community institutions to enact secondary legislation with binding force. Consider what would happen if a piece of secondary legislation was enacted which was deficient in some way. Without some mechanism through which to challenge its legality, it would remain in force. Article 230 EC therefore allows an action for judicial review to be taken before the ECJ, which has the competence to examine the measure in question. The procedure outlined in Art 230 EC is in essence an action for *annulment* of the contested act. In the event that the applicant is successful in their action, the ECJ has the power under Art 231 EC to declare the act *void*.

As a complement to the judicial review process, it is also possible under Art 288(2) EC for individuals to seek damages from the Community for non-contractual loss caused by either the institutions or their servants. The competence of the Community courts to hear such actions is outlined in Art 235 EC.

## WHICH ACTS OF THE COMMUNITY MAY BE REVIEWED?

Article 230(1) EC details that the Court of Justice (and, by reason of Art 225 EC, the Court of First Instance as well) may review the legality of the following:

- Acts adopted jointly by the European Parliament and the Council;
- Acts of the Council;
- Acts of the Commission;
- Acts of the European Central Bank;
- Acts of the European Parliament.

The list above quite clearly includes the most common legislative acts produced by the Community institutions, which are Regulations, Directives and Decisions. While other acts are capable of judicial review, they must be intended to generate legal effects in respect of third parties. What this means is that recommendations, opinions and other acts which are not binding upon other parties are not generally capable of review. The acts which may be subject to review will, however, be widened considerably if the Treaty of Lisbon is adopted.

## ON WHAT GROUNDS MAY AN ACTION FOR ANNULMENT BE TAKEN?

If an individual wishes to challenge the legality of a legislative act of the Community, it would not be sufficient for them merely to assert that they do not like the contents of the act. Rather, the applicant would have to give reasons for their challenge to the legality of the particular legislative act at issue. The reasons which the Court will accept as a legitimate base for an action for judicial review are listed in Art 230(2) EC. These can be summarised as follows:

- Under Art 7 EC, each Community institution must act within the limits of its powers. As such, there must be a legal basis within the Treaties for every legal act adopted. If a Community institution were to enact legislation in an area outside of its powers, the act in question could be annulled *for lack of competence.*
- *Infringement of an essential procedural requirement.* This ground is applicable to situations in which the correct procedure has not been followed in enacting the act in question.
- *Infringement of the Treaty or any rule of law relating to the application of the Treaty.* An action for annulment may be taken if the contested act

infringes provisions of any of the Treaties or binding legislation made under them. Furthermore, this ground also permits review on the basis that the act in question infringes one of the general principles of Community law.

- *Misuse of powers.* The Community and its institutions are granted powers to achieve particular aims. Misuse of powers refers to the scenario under which such powers are exercised to achieve a purpose which is not linked to the reasons for which the power was initially granted. This ground of challenge is rarely successful though there have been some instances in which the Court has annulled a measure for misuse of powers: *Simmenthal* v *Commission* (Case 92/78).

## IS THERE A TIME LIMIT APPLICABLE TO AN ACTION FOR JUDICIAL REVIEW?

The time limit for an action for annulment is 2 months and runs from the date of publication of the act in the *Official Journal* or from its notification to the applicant. In the absence of either of these events, the time limit starts to run as soon as the applicant becomes aware of the act.

## WHAT HAPPENS IF AN APPLICANT IS SUCCESSFUL IN THEIR ACTION FOR ANNULMENT?

The consequences of a successful action for annulment are outlined in Art 231 EC:

"1 If the action is well founded, the Court of Justice shall declare the act concerned to be void.

2. In the case of a regulation, however, the Court of Justice shall, if it considers this necessary, state which of the effects of the regulation which it has declared void shall be considered to be definitive."

Thus, following a successful action for annulment, the ECJ has the competence to declare an act of the Community, or a part of that act, void. In the case of a Regulation, the ECJ may, however, pronounce certain components of it operational.

## CAN ANYONE BRING AN ACTION FOR ANNULMENT OF A COMMUNITY ACT?

In most domestic legal systems, an action for judicial review may be taken only by someone who has "standing" or *locus standi* to do so. This is in essence a requirement that one must establish a legal connection with the contested act before the Court will give permission for the validity of the act to be challenged. There are three categories of applicant listed under Art 230 EC as having standing to bring an action for judicial review:

- Member States, the European Parliament, the Council and the Commission will always have sufficient standing to challenge the validity of an act. They are hence referred to as "*privileged applications*".

- The Court of Auditors and the European Central Bank are "*semi-privileged applicants*". They only have standing to protect their prerogatives. Under the Treaty of Lisbon, the Committee of the Regions is introduced as a semi-privileged applicant.

- Natural and legal persons may challenge the validity of a Community act but only if they can satisfy a number of requirements. Natural and legal persons are referred to as "*non-privileged applicants*".

## WHAT REQUIREMENTS MUST NON-PRIVILEGED APPLICANTS SATISFY IN ORDER TO BRING AN ACTION FOR JUDICIAL REVIEW?

Article 230(4) EC provides:

> "Any natural or legal persons may ... institute proceedings against a decision addressed to that person or against a decision which, although in the form of a regulation or a decision addressed to another person, is of direct and individual concern to the former."

We will deal with each of these situations in turn:

### A decision addressed to the applicant

An individual who is the addressee of a decision will generally always have standing to challenge the validity of the act in question.

### A decision which is in the form of a Regulation

The authority to enact Regulations is provided for by Art 249 EC, which sets out that Regulations are "generally applicable". Initially, the ECJ held that private individuals *could not* challenge the validity of a Regulation. This is because Art 230(4) requires the applicant to establish "direct and individual concern" in order to have standing. As such, it was reasoned that a legislative instrument which has general application could not at the same time be of direct and individual concern to an individual. However, the Community courts now recognise that a Regulation *can in fact* be both generally and individually applicable. As such, the provisions of a Regulation are challengeable so long as they are of "direct and individual concern" to the applicant: *Calpak* v *Commission* (Cases 789 and 790/79) .

## A decision addressed to someone else

If a decision is addressed to "another person", it may be challenged by a non-privileged applicant if they can show that it is of "direct and individual" concern to them.

The requirement to establish direct and individual concern is thus common to the latter two categories of non-privileged applicants. The ECJ has elaborated upon the meaning to be given to each of these terms since no definition was provided in the EC Treaty.

## WHAT IS DIRECT CONCERN?

In order to establish direct concern, applicants must show that the relevant measure *directly affects* their legal situation. In addition, there must be no intervening act between the passing of the measure and its impact on the applicant. If a Member State is required to take implementing measures to incorporate the provisions of the contested act into national law, then there must be no discretion granted with regard to how to implement them. Essentially, there must be a direct and uninterrupted causal link between the measure concerned and its impact upon the applicant: see, for example, *Les Verts* v *Parliament* (Case 294/83).

Normally the issue of direct concern is looked at by the Community courts *after* the applicant has established they have individual concern in the measure. That is because the test of individual concern is such that most non-privileged applicants (that is, natural and legal persons) do not pass it.

## WHAT IS INDIVIDUAL CONCERN?: THE *"PLAUMANN* TEST"

The test which the Community courts use in establishing whether the applicant has individual concern in the contested measure was set out in *Plaumann* v *Commission* (Case 25/62). Plaumann was an importer of clementines from outside the European Community and, as such, had to pay a 13 per cent tariff on his imports. He wanted to challenge the legality of a decision taken by the Commission to retain the tariff and argued that, as one of the few importers of clementines into the Community, he was directly and individually concerned by the decision of the Commission not to repeal the tariff.

The ECJ held that while Plaumann's commercial interests were impacted upon by the Commission's decision to retain the tariff, he could not be classed as being individually concerned by it. This was because the commercial activity in which he was engaged was the type which anyone could practise at any given time. He was thus a member of an "open class" of individuals and could not distinguish himself from others who could potentially engage in the same activity. He was thus not granted standing to challenge the decision.

The ECJ held that in order for non-privileged applicants to establish "individual concern" in a decision which is not addressed to them, it is necessary for them to demonstrate:

> "[T]hat the decision affects them by reason of certain attributes which are peculiar to them or by reason of circumstances in which they are differentiated from all other persons and by virtue of those factors distinguishes them individually just as in the case of the person addressed. In the present case, the applicant is affected by the disputed decision as an importer of clementines, that is to say, by reason of a commercial activity which may or may not be practised by any person and is not therefore such as to distinguish the applicant in relation to the contested Decision as in the case of an addressee."

The *Plaumann* test for "individual concern" may be expressed as follows:

- the applicant is affected by the decision by reason of certain characteristics which are particular to them; *or*
- the applicant is affected by the decision by reason of circumstances by which the applicant is differentiated from all other persons.

It is evident that the "test" for individual concern set out by the Court in the case of *Plaumann* is extremely restrictive. The problem with such a narrow test for individual concern is that it effectively excludes a myriad of applicants from availing themselves of the judicial review procedure. The approach of the Court in this regard has been heavily criticised, particularly in relation to how the rules impact upon the rights of public interest groups to litigate on behalf of groups of individuals.

## JUDICIAL REVIEW AND INTEREST GROUPS

The European political process actively encourages the involvement of certain non-governmental organisations in the policy-making process. This is particularly so in relation to areas of decision making which are comprised within the "new governance" agenda within the European Union.

However, one area of Community law in which interest groups are not so well represented is in relation to standing under Art 230 EC. Interest groups are treated as non-privileged applicants and are hence required to prove "direct and individual" concern before they may have standing. The restrictiveness of the *Plaumann* test for individual concern means that it is almost impossible for an interest group ever to have standing to bring an action for judicial review of a Community act.

However, interest groups provide an important democratic function as their existence ensures that a range of views are expressed in the political arena. Many domestic legal systems permit interest groups to take an action for judicial review on behalf of a group of individuals. This allows individuals who may not otherwise be able to fund an action for judicial review to pool their resources with other citizens who share the same concerns. The restrictive approach taken to standing under Art 230 EC explicitly precludes such a possibility since it will generally be impossible for a large group of people sharing the same concern all to have *individual* concern in the law in question.

The problems inherent in this approach are perhaps best exemplified in *Stichting Greenpeace Council (Greenpeace International)* v *Commission* (Case T-585/93). In this case, Greenpeace challenged a Commission decision granting aid to Spain to build two power stations on the Canary Islands. Greenpeace challenged the measure on the basis that the projects did not comply with Community environmental policy. Its challenge had the support of a significant number of Canary Islands residents as well as other interested parties such as tourists and environmentalists. The Court of First Instance held that none of the applicants had direct and individual concern under the test established in the case of *Plaumann*:

> "It has consistently been held that an association formed for the protection of the collective interests of a category of persons cannot be considered to be directly and individually concerned ... by a measure affecting the general interests of that category, and is therefore not entitled to bring an action for annulment where its members may not do so individually."

On appeal to the ECJ in *Stichting Greenpeace Council (Greenpeace International)* v *Commission* (Case C–321/95 P), Greenpeace argued that special rules should be established for standing in relation to environmental matters. The ECJ disagreed and upheld the original decision of the Court of First Instance not to grant standing. The outcome of the judgment was effectively to bar any challenge to the building of the two power stations since it was impossible for anyone to establish individual concern in the Commission's decision to grant funding to the projects.

The rules on standing were subsequently re-examined by the Court in the case of *Union de Pequeños Agricultores* v *Council* (2002) (*"UPA* case"). The case concerned a request for annulment of a Regulation with-drawing aid to olive oil producers. As a Regulation, no national implementing measures were required to bring it into effect. National rules, however, precluded its legality from being called into question in proceedings before the applicants' national court. Unless the applicants were granted standing under Art 230(4), they would be deprived of any avenue of redress to change the legality of the contested Regulation.

The ECJ commenced its judgment by noting that the Community is one based upon the "rule of law". Central to this was the recognition accorded to the right of effective judicial protection which

> "is one of the general principles of law stemming from the constitutional traditions common to the Member States ... The Treaty has established a complete system of legal remedies and procedures designed to ensure judicial review of the legality of acts of the institutions ... Under that system, where natural and legal persons cannot, by reason of the conditions for admissibility laid down in fourth paragraph of [Article 230 EC] of the Treaty, directly challenge Community measures of general application, they are able, depending upon the case ... to do so before the national courts and ask them ... to make a reference to the Court of Justice for a preliminary ruling on validity".

In the case of *UPA*, the ECJ therefore recognised that the right to effective judicial protection is an essential component of the Community legal system. However, it held that a complete system of legal protection had been developed in Community law through the interaction of the judicial review process under Art 230 EC and the preliminary reference procedure outlined by Art 234 EC. According to the ECJ, where an applicant was denied standing under Art 230(4), they could revert to the fall-back mechanism of asking their national court to make a preliminary reference request on the legality of the act in question to the Community courts.

Thus, in the view of the ECJ, if applicants were denied direct access to the Community courts under Art 230 EC, they could still gain *indirect access* (albeit through their national courts) via the operation of the preliminary reference procedure. Where national rules prevented the applicants challenging the validity of Community acts, it was not for the ECJ to change the rules on standing. Rather, it was noted by the ECJ as being "for the Member States to establish a system of legal remedies and procedures which ensure respect for the right to effective judicial protection".

The reasoning of the ECJ in *UPA* was followed by the ECJ in *Jego-Quere* v *Commission* (Case T 177/01). In this later case, the ECJ held that while the right to effective legal protection was central to the Community legal order, this had been established through a combination of the judicial review and preliminary reference procedure. Again, on the facts at issue in the case of *Jego-Quere*, it was clear that the domestic legal system *did not provide* the applicants with an opportunity to contest the validity of the Regulation at issue and so a preliminary reference request via the applicant's national courts was not possible. However, the ECJ said it could not extend the rules on standing under Art 230(4).

## CONCLUSION

The rules on standing in relation to non-privileged applicants have been criticised in many quarters. Given the position of the Court in relation to these rules, it is apparent that a Treaty amendment will be required before natural and legal persons will acquire *locus standi* to lodge an application for judicial review under Art 230 EC. Such an amendment has been proposed under the Treaty of Lisbon such that, if the Treaty becomes law, the provision on standing to commence judicial review proceedings would read as follows:

"Any natural or legal person may institute proceedings ... against an act addressed to that person or which is of direct and individual concern to him or her, and against a regulatory act which is of direct concern to him or her and does not entail implementing measures." (Art 263 TFEU)

The main change to the judicial review procedure under the Treaty of Lisbon relates to the capacity of a private person to challenge the legality of a regulatory act which is only of "direct concern" to him or her. However, such a challenge can only be made in the event that the act in question does not require implementing measures. Whether this amendment has the capacity to bring about a significant widening of access to the judicial review process remains to be seen.

## Essential Facts

- The procedure outlined in Art 230 EC is akin to "judicial review".

- Any act of the Community institutions which produces legal effects in relation to third parties is potentially reviewable.

- Applicants for judicial review have to adhere to strict time limits to challenge the provisions of an act.

- There are three categories of applicant under Art 230 EC:
    - privileged applicants, who will always have standing;
    - semi-privileged applicants, who will have standing to protect their prerogatives;
    - non-privileged applicants, who have to establish "direct and individual concern" so as to gain standing under judicial review procedure.

- It is extremely difficult for private individuals to challenge the legality of Community action directly before the Community courts.

- For non-privileged applicants to challenge the legality of a Community act (which is not addressed to them), it is necessary for them to establish that they are directly and individually concerned by the measure in question.

- A Community act will be of "direct" concern to a non-privileged applicant where it "directly" affects the legal situation of the applicant and leaves no room to the addressee of the measure who is tasked with its implementation.

- A Community act will be of "individual" concern to a non-privileged applicant where the act "affects them by reason of certain attributes which are peculiar to them or by reason of circumstances in which they are differentiated from all other persons".

- The ECJ has the competence under Art 231 EC to declare an act of the Community institutions void should an action for judicial review prove successful.

**Essential Cases**

**Plaumann v Commission (1963)**: in order for a non-privileged applicant to satisfy the test for individual concern, they must be able to demonstrate that the act in question affects them in a manner which is differentiated from all other persons.

**Stichting Greenpeace Council (Greenpeace International) v Commission (1998)**: there are no special rules in place to facilitate the access of interest groups to the judicial review process.

**Union de Pequeños Agricultores v Council (2002)**: effective judicial protection is provided through the interaction of Art 230 EC and Art 234 EC.

# 11 WHAT NEXT?

## LOOKING TO THE FUTURE?

The European Union of today is markedly different from the functional grouping of countries which combined to form the European Economic Community. Both the aim and scope of the constituent Treaties of the European Union are far beyond those envisaged by the "founding fathers" of the European integration project. The aim of this chapter is to look to the future and provide a brief overview of issues which are likely to influence European policy making in the short to medium term.

### The Treaty of Lisbon

The first issue which is likely to dominate the European agenda in the coming year is the question of what to do with the Treaty of Lisbon. Most Member States have now ratified the Treaty and so it is likely that increasing pressure will be put upon the Irish Government to hold another referendum on the issue. At the time of writing, it is probable that another vote will be held in 2009, although it is not immediately obvious whether the Irish electorate will overturn the results of the first referendum. However, various "sweeteners" have been offered in order to increase the likelihood of Irish ratification. These include the introduction of rules such that the number of Commissioners will not decrease, with the consequence that there will remain at least one Commissioner for each Member State. Additional guarantees have been offered to ensure that Ireland is able to retain its military neutrality and provisions have been proposed to ensure that Ireland's stance on issues such as abortion is not affected by the introduction of the Treaty of Lisbon. These guarantees are likely to be appended to Croatia's Treaty of Accession which will be drawn up whenever it accedes to the European Union.

### Expansion

The accession of Croatia to the European Union will bring the number of Member States up to 28. However, whether the Union will continue to expand much more beyond this is unclear. This is because the recent expansion of the EU precipitated a wave of migrant workers flocking to the "old" EU Member States. As a consequence, a series of transitional restrictions were placed on such migration by a number of the older Member States. These restrictions are permitted under the rules governing the accession of the "new" Member States but may be imposed only temporarily. One of the concerns surrounding the future expansion of Europe to include countries such as Turkey is the sheer size of Turkey's population which currently stands at over 70 million people. Such apprehension stems from disquiet as to the economic ramifications of further enlargement of the Union. This is particularly so given the current economic climate.

## The economy

At the time of writing, the world is recognised to be in recession. The EU has not escaped unscathed from the flurry of economic turmoil which has resulted from this, with various eastern European countries recently having sought assistance from the International Monetary Fund. As a consequence, there is increasing pressure upon the EU as a whole to formulate a plan to lift the Union out of recession. This has resulted in agreement between the leaders of the EU Member States that more must be done to regulate global financial markets. In the coming years, it is likely that much energy will be exerted by EU policy makers to tighten global financial rules.

## The environment

Another pressing concern which requires an EU-level response is the environment. Central to the environmental agenda of the EU over the next few years is the need to combat the effects of climate change. As a consequence, the EU as a whole has committed to reduce carbon emissions 20 per cent below 1990 levels by 2020. As a complement to this, agreement has also been reached to secure a 20 per cent share for renewable energy by 2020.

## CONCLUSION

The European Union of today is a remarkably different entity than the loose economic grouping envisaged by the founding fathers of the Treaty of Rome. Over the years, its competence and "vision" have changed considerably, with the consequence that Europe today stands at something of a crossroads as to the future direction of its policy making and politics. However, the expansion of the competence of the European Union has to some extent been to the detriment of its popular legitimacy. The failure of the Irish electorate to ratify the Treaty of Lisbon is perhaps something of a testament to the failure of the European project to engage more fully with its citizens. In the difficult years ahead, there also must be a concerted effort to move decision making closer to European citizens. Only time will tell whether this goal will be achieved.

# INDEX